# Women, Crime, and Criminal Justice

**Ralph Weisheit**
**Sue Mahan**

**CJ** Criminal Justice Studies
Anderson Publishing Co.
Cincinnati, Ohio

WOMEN, CRIME, AND CRIMINAL JUSTICE

**Library of Congress Catalog Number**  87-070601

**ISBN**  0-932930-77-8

Kelly Humble *Managing Editor*

Cover design by James Simon

## DEDICATION

To Carol—my best friend, wife, and constant source of support.—RW

To a special father, Frank V. Maurer, who proved that there is an exception
for every rule—even the rule of patriarchy!—SM

# CONTENTS

# Introduction

Since the mid-1970s social science research has reflected a tremendous interest in issues facing women. It should not be surprising that the study of crime, which draws on a number of disciplines, has also reflected this heightened sensitivity to women's issues. Prior to 1970, introductory criminology and criminal justice texts paid scant attention to the issue of female criminality, but by the mid-1980s this had all changed as academic interest in the subject grew. Further, those who worked in criminal justice agencies wanted to learn as much as possible about women in criminal justice to protect themselves from lawsuits based on charges of discrimination.

In the past decade, a growing number of universities have begun offering courses in female criminality. Consistent with the broad-based interest of both academics and criminal justice practitioners, these courses have focused on three primary issues: women as offenders, women as victims, and women as criminal justice employees. This text has been organized around these three primary issues, but material about women in prison, in court, and information about women who commit crimes in other cultures has also been included.

There are several excellent books on female criminality, but they are relatively focused in content area, or are edited books, and hence lack the integration of materials and breadth of coverage possible in a survey text. This text has been written in response to the growing need for a book which can be used both as a text in Women and Crime courses and as a reference guide by those who wish to familiarize themselves with the major issues and research findings related to female criminality. The chapter on the victimization of women provides a summary of the countless articles and publications about incest, rape, battering and harassment which have come out in recent years. It is hoped that this chapter will spark the interest of readers and act as a catalyst for more study of victimology. For that reason, an extensive bibliography has been included with Chapter 5 as an aid for students and researchers.

In many ways, the kind of book presented here could not have been written ten years ago. The extensive study of female criminality is so recent that many of the key issues are only now becoming clear. But several themes persisted throughout the widely divergent subject areas covered in this book. First, the roles of women as criminals, victims and employees have not undergone a radical transformation since the 1960s. The rhetoric of liberation does not reflect the continued pattern of defining women as second-class citizens. Second, the involvement of women in criminal activity, victimization, and criminal justice employment is strongly linked to the role of women in society. None of these issues can be studied in isolation from larger social roles and institutions outside of criminal justice.

Finally, improving our understanding of women's participation in these three areas will also improve our understanding of crime and criminal justice more generally. Here are some examples: the successful utilization of women as patrol officers in major police departments has raised serious questions about how police performance is properly measured and about the importance of height and weight restrictions on new recruits; prisons for women have often been used as laboratories for studying prison policies and programs before they are put into effect elsewhere in the system; and attention to the needs of women who are victims of crimes of sexual exploitation has led to more attention to victimology in the entire criminal justice process.

Above all, it is our hope that this book sensitizes the reader to the variety and complexity of issues raised when studying women in the criminal justice system. By focusing on women, it is possible to gain insights into the larger criminal justice system and into society itself.

# 1

# The "New"
# Female Offender

## Introduction

Females have long been involved in criminal activity. In fact, some of the most notorious criminals in history have been women. Consider the following examples from the United States:

LIZZIE BORDEN. In August of 1892, Lizzie Borden's father and step-mother were brutally hacked to death with an unknown sharp instrument, probably an ax. Although she was acquitted of the murders, there were no other suspects and it is still believed by many that Lizzie was responsible.

It has been speculated that she was motivated by a fear that her step-mother would persuade Lizzie's wealthy father to change his will, largely excluding Lizzie and her sister Emma (Spierling, 1984).

BELLE GUNNESS. Described by one author as the "Lady Bluebeard," Belle Gunness has been listed in the Guiness Book of World Records for committing more murders than any woman in history, with some estimating as many as 30 victims. She bought a farm in LaPorte, Indiana in 1901, using insurance money from the mysterious death of her first husband a year earlier. Within a year her second husband died, and she placed ads in lonely hearts columns for male suitors. In 1908 a fire struck her farm; in the ruins were found the remains of numerous men, three women and three children, most of whom were buried in the gardens and hog pens on the farm. It is believed that she died in the fire (probably a suicide), but some speculate that the burned remains were of another woman and that Belle herself had gone to California (Langlois, 1985).

BONNIE PARKER. Bonnie Parker and Clyde Barrow, Bonnie and Clyde, were primarily known for a string of bank robberies in the midwestern United States in the 1930s. They were fascinated with weapons and killed at least 15 people, most of whom were police officers. As one author has noted, "They loved killing and robbing and had no scruples whatsoever....Both were neurotic about weapons and thrilled to possess and fire them. To obtain any high powered automatic weapon meant ecstasy for the couple (Nash, 1981, p. 318)." The couple was killed in 1934 in a police ambush in which their car was riddled with more than two hundred bullets.

ARIZONA "MA" BARKER. In the 1930s Ma Barker led her four sons and occasional male companions in bank robbery, kidnapping, and murder. She was adept at the use of weapons and died in a shootout with police in 1935. It has been alleged that Ma had her sons and male companions procure young girls for homosexual abuse, after which she would order the girls killed (Nash, 1981).

While female criminals have existed for some time, it is only in recent years that systematic attention has been focused on this offender group. Most of our early explanations of crime and descriptions of criminals have been based on studies of male offenders. In the mid 1970s, however, this was to change. Newspaper accounts, often based on the observations of police officers, judges, or prison officials told of a new breed of female offender whose penchant for violence and aggression rivaled that of males. Scholars studying the crime problem also began to focus their attention on the female offender.

In 1975 two books were published which set the stage for much of the debate on female criminality for the next decade. Freda Adler's book, *Sisters In Crime*, echoed the popular view that female criminality was increasingly violent, and that much of this change could be traced directly to the rise of the women's movement. Liberation was a two-edged sword, freeing women to engage in both legitimate and illegitimate activities traditionally reserved for men. Women began to realize, for example, that a pressing need for money could be met by armed robbery or burglary. Adler conducted no systematic tests of her arguments, but relied on anecdotal material.  Nevertheless, her work was instrumental in drawing attention to the issue of female criminality.  A second pivotal book published in 1975 was Rita Simon's *Women and Crime*.  Simon used arrest and court records to argue that female criminality was on the rise, but only for *property* offenses.  She suggested that increases in property crime were a logical consequence of more women entering the labor market and having greater access to situations in which this type of crime was possible.

The works of Adler and of Simon brought the problem of female criminality to the attention of criminologists, who have come to realize that an understanding of female criminality may broaden our understanding of crime in general.  In this chapter attention will be directed at various explanations of female criminality.  Before this, however, it is essential to describe the nature and extent of criminality by women, and to compare it with that of men.

## Nature of Female Criminality

The major source of data which may be used to describe female criminality is that provided by official police records.  Although the problems with official data are well known (O'Brien, 1985), such records are the only sources of information which:  (1) provide at least basic information on the characteristics of offenders, (2) are national in scope, and (3) have been routinely collected over a number of years.  For these reasons, much of our discussion will be based on police statistics.

Each year the FBI collects information about criminal offenders from approximately 10,000 police agencies throughout the United States and publishes this information in the *Uniform Crime Reports* (UCR).  For 1984, information was provided for 28 specific offenses, ranging in seriousness from murder to vagrancy.  An examination of these data reveals that both in absolute terms and when compared with males, female criminality is overwhelmingly nonviolent.  In fact, the crimes of murder and robbery combined account for only *six tenths of one percent* of all female arrests.

However, as Steffensmeier (1978) has argued, simply comparing the *number* of male and female offenders in each offense category may lead to inaccurate conclusions, since there are more females than males in the overall population.  To adjust for these population differences, rates per 100,000 were computed here for each offense type.  That is, the number of crimes are reported as if there were only 100,000 males and 100,000 females in the population.

TABLE 1.1

Ten Offenses for Which Females Were Most Often Arrested
in 1984, with Rates of Arrest for Each Sex.

|  | Adjusted Rate Per 100,000[a] | |
| --- | --- | --- |
| Offense | Female Rate | Male Rate |
| 1. Larceny-Theft[b] | 380.0 | 959.9 |
| 2. Driving Under the Influence | 194.3 | 1621.4 |
| 3. Disorderly Conduct | 110.5 | 579.8 |
| 4. Fraud[c] | 102.2 | 165.0 |
| 5. Drug Law Violations | 97.4 | 659.3 |
| 6. Drunkenness | 95.2 | 1103.0 |
| 7. Runaways[d] | 82.4 | 65.6 |
| 8. Liquor Law Violations | 78.5 | 436.1 |
| 9. Simple Assault[e] | 77.1 | 471.9 |
| 10. Prostitution/Vice | 76.9 | 36.3 |

[a] Based on formula presented by Steffensmeier (1978) which takes into account the fact that UCR data does not include the entire population and that there are more females than males in the population.

[b] Includes shoplifting, pocket-picking, or other kinds of theft which do not involve force or fraud.

[c] Includes such offenses as writing bad checks.

[d] Limited to juveniles.

[e] Assault in which no weapon was used or which did not result in serious injury to the victim.

Table 1.1 shows the 10 offenses for which females are most often arrested, with the corresponding rates of offending for both sexes. As the table shows, even the most frequent offenses by females are rare when compared with those of males. Only running away and prostitution are more often reported for females, and both of these offenses are unique, having been defined by some as "victimless" crimes. Victimless crimes are those in which the "victim" and offender are one and the same, leading some to argue that the harm resulting from the crime is often less than that from its legal enforcement (cf. Schur & Bedau, 1974). In fact, when drug law violations, drunkenness, and liquor law violations are included among victimless crimes, half of the top ten female crimes are victimless crimes. In short, the crimes for which women are most frequently arrested are of a relatively minor nature, are decidedly non-violent, and are often those in which the women themselves are the primary "victims."

TABLE 1.2
Index Crimes for 1984, with Rates of Arrest for Each Sex.

| Offense | Adjusted Rate Per 100,000[a] | |
| --- | --- | --- |
| | Female Rate | Male Rate |
| VIOLENT CRIMES | | |
| Murder | 2.3 | 16.1 |
| Rape | .3 | 38.2 |
| Robbery | 9.8 | 137.2 |
| Aggravated Assault | 38.6 | 273.3 |
| PROPERTY CRIMES | | |
| Burglary | 30.7 | 421.9 |
| Larceny-Theft | 380.0 | 959.9 |
| Motor Vehicle Theft | 10.7 | 115.4 |
| Arson | 2.2 | 16.1 |

[a] Based on formula presented by Steffensmeier (1978) which takes into account the fact that UCR data does not include the entire population and that there are more females than males in the population.

What about serious crime?  The UCR data identifies eight offenses as "Index Crimes."  These are among the most serious offenses and are generally used when discussing trends over time in crime.  There are two major categories of Index Crime, violent crimes (murder, rape, robbery, aggravated assault) and property crimes (larceny-theft, burglary, motor vehicle theft, and arson).  Table 1.2 compares male and female rates of arrest for each of these Index Crimes for 1984.  The table reveals several important points about serious crimes listed among the Index Offenses.  First, both males and females are more likely to be arrested for property crimes than for violent crimes.  Second, there is no serious crime for which females are more often arrested than males.  In fact, for several of the offenses the differences between male and female rates are striking.  For example, males are nearly 14 times more often arrested for burglary or robbery, and are 7 times more often arrested for murder or aggravated assault.  Finally, among property and violent crimes the patterns for males and females are similar.  That is, those crimes for which males are most often arrested are also those for which females are most often arrested.  This finding is supported by self-report studies of delinquency (Canter, 1982; Hindelang, 1971; Mawby, 1980; Richards, 1981).

## Changes Over Time

The sudden interest in female criminality spawned in the mid-1970s was based on two beliefs about female criminality.  First, it was thought that female criminality was on the rise and might at some point reach numerical and qualitative parity with male criminality.  Second, many believed that this change was directly tied to the emancipation of women, and might well portend the rise of other problems as the social roles of men and women changed.  The merits of these arguments and of specific explanations for female criminality will be examined in the next section.  At this point, it is essential to first describe the extent to which female criminality has changed over time by focusing particular attention on offenses which might be related to emancipation.

The first question is whether the *character* or nature of female criminality has changed.  In particular, has female criminality become increasingly violent?  Examining Index Offenses from 1965-1984 (excluding rape because it is primarily a male offense and arson because it has only been included among Index offenses since 1979) we find that the percentage of Index Crimes which are crimes of violence remains surprisingly stable for both males and females.  About 11 percent of Index Crimes committed by females are crimes of violence, while for males about 21 percent are crimes of violence.  In other words, nearly twice as many of the Index Crimes committed by males were crimes of violence and this figure has remained relatively constant over the past 20 years.  In fact, the highest percentages of violent crimes for females are in 1965 and 1966, where more than 13 percent of Index crimes are crimes of violence.  These data suggest little support for the argument that female criminality is increasingly violent.

A second question is whether the *amount* of female criminality has changed over time, particularly regarding specific offenses.  For example, it might be argued that the growing number of women in the workplace would lead to a rise in embezzlement, or that as women become more involved in the social world outside of the home they will more frequently engage in such crimes as aggravated assault.  Table 1.3 shows male and female arrest rates for four selected offenses for the years 1965-1984.  The table includes two crimes of violence (aggravated assault and robbery), and two property crimes (burglary, and embezzlement).

It is interesting to note that the crime most directly linked to occupational roles, embezzlement, is also the most stable.   Rates of embezzling change relatively little over the years, and certainly show no continuous dramatic increase among females.  From Table 1.3, it is not difficult to see how writers in the mid-1970s saw rather consistent increases in such crimes as assault, robbery, and burglary.  Most of these writers used a rather limited time frame, comparing data from the late 1960s with those from the early and mid-1970s to assess the impact of the women's movement on female criminality.  With the benefit of an additional ten years of data, however, we can see that the increase for robbery and burglary has pretty well leveled off, although the rate of aggravated assault continues a general pattern of increase.  This is consistent with Smart's (1979) observations based on British data from the 1930s through the 1970s.  She noted that there were considerable fluctuations in female criminality over time, with no unilateral increases in general female criminality.

Thus, for robbery, burglary, and embezzlement there are serious doubts about the assumption that female criminality is on a steady upward spiral.  Further, while male rates of embezzlement have declined over time, the rates for assault, robbery, and burglary have risen even more for males than for females.  For example, nearly 16 more women per 100,000 were arrested for aggravated assault between 1966 and 1984.  For men the number increased by 112 arrests per 100,000 males in the population.  Thus, even where female criminality has risen steadily, the increase is small compared to that for males.  From these data one would be hard pressed to argue that male and female rates are converging.  The only offense listed for which there is convergence is embezzlement, and in this case the

TABLE 1.3
Adjusted Rate of Crime/100,000 for Selected Offenses, 1965-1984.[a]

| Year | Aggravated Assault | | Robbery | | Burglary | | Embezzlement | |
|------|------|--------|------|--------|------|--------|------|--------|
|      | Male | Female | Male | Female | Male | Female | Male | Female |
| 1965 | 142.0 | 21.0 | 84.6 | 4.4 | 370.4 | 13.5 | 12.4 | 2.4 |
| 1966 | 161.2 | 23.0 | 84.3 | 4.2 | 362.5 | 13.7 | 9.8 | 2.2 |
| 1967 | 166.0 | 23.0 | 100.8 | 5.2 | 408.5 | 16.2 | 8.7 | 1.9 |
| 1968 | 165.6 | 21.9 | 115.8 | 6.4 | 436.0 | 17.7 | 8.4 | 1.9 |
| 1969 | 177.3 | 23.8 | 128.0 | 7.9 | 436.7 | 18.5 | 8.9 | 2.2 |
| 1970 | 184.4 | 24.8 | 138.0 | 8.3 | 455.8 | 20.8 | 10.3 | 3.1 |
| 1971 | 197.3 | 28.1 | 154.5 | 9.7 | 486.1 | 23.4 | 8.7 | 2.7 |
| 1972 | 210.6 | 29.9 | 159.2 | 10.3 | 464.9 | 23.6 | 7.8 | 2.6 |
| 1973 | 215.4 | 30.7 | 152.3 | 10.3 | 479.7 | 25.4 | 6.9 | 2.0 |
| 1974 | 246.2 | 35.6 | 186.1 | 12.7 | 593.1 | 31.7 | 8.0 | 2.7 |
| 1975 | 240.9 | 33.7 | 165.3 | 11.7 | 582.0 | 31.2 | 8.8 | 3.7 |
| 1976 | 233.3 | 32.8 | 142.7 | 10.2 | 537.1 | 27.7 | 7.9 | 3.3 |
| 1977 | 237.2 | 32.5 | 139.4 | 10.4 | 524.8 | 31.3 | 6.3 | 1.7 |
| 1978 | 264.6 | 35.7 | 154.7 | 10.9 | 536.1 | 32.7 | 6.8 | 2.1 |
| 1979 | 266.9 | 35.2 | 143.8 | 10.7 | 520.6 | 32.8 | 7.0 | 2.2 |
| 1980 | 264.8 | 34.8 | 151.2 | 10.9 | 525.7 | 32.1 | 6.6 | 2.4 |
| 1981 | 266.2 | 35.1 | 142.9 | 12.1 | 523.6 | 32.0 | 6.7 | 2.4 |
| 1982 | 294.3 | 39.9 | 167.1 | 12.0 | 532.0 | 34.3 | 6.7 | 2.7 |
| 1983 | 275.6 | 39.4 | 151.4 | 11.0 | 472.4 | 31.4 | 6.3 | 2.7 |
| 1984 | 273.3 | 38.6 | 137.2 | 9.8 | 421.9 | 30.7 | 5.4 | 2.9 |

[a] Based on formula presented by Steffensmeier (1978) which takes into account the fact that UCR data does not include the entire population and that there are more females than males in the population.

convergence is not due to an increase in female criminality, but to a *decrease* in the arrest of males. These figures, particularly those for embezzling, also raise serious questions about the impact of women's liberation. Either the emancipation of women occurred on a much smaller scale than has been assumed by those who study women and crime, or emancipation has little impact on the extent of involvement in criminality by women.

## Convergence Reconsidered

As we have noted, there are serious questions about the extent to which male and female rates have converged over time. Some have approached the issue of convergence from a quite different perspective. Rather than looking at male/female differences over time, they have examined differences across social groups. For example, in his classic economic study of crime, Bonger (1916) argued that sex differences in criminality would be greater in the upper classes since lower-class men and women were more similar in their "manner of life." More recently, Hagan et al. (1985) have provided empirical support for Bonger's arguments by showing that lower-class males and females are more similar in their delinquency than are upper-class males and females. Hagan (1985) also used the logic of this argument to account for sex differences by racial groups. In his study of Canadian inmates he found that differences between minority and majority group crime rates were greater for men than for women and that male/female differences in crime were smaller in minority groups. These differences, he argued, were due to the relative social position of both females and minorities in society. Thus, the work of Bonger and of Hagan and his associates have suggested what may prove to be a far more fruitful approach to the study of convergence. And, as will be discussed later in this chapter, Hagan et al. (1985) were able to use these ideas to construct a plausible theory to account for male-female differences in criminality.

## Describing The Female Offender

Since the early 1970s there have been several hundred published studies of the female offender, usually focusing on the extent of female criminality compared with that of males, the nature of female criminality, or factors associated with female criminality. It may, therefore, be somewhat surprising that very little has been published which *describes* characteristics of female offenders themselves. Most descriptive studies are also limited in that they: (1) focus on special offender groups (such as homicide offenders, robbers, or prostitutes), (2) have been based on descriptions of prison populations, which clearly represent a group of offenders who have survived a rather extensive screening process, or (3) have been self-report studies which almost exclusively focus on adolescents and relatively minor offenses. There is at least one notable exception to this general pattern.  Wolfe, Cullen, and  Cullen (1984) used police records on 2,507 female arrestees in a southern city for the years 1969-1975 to portray the female offender. They made observations about the following variables:

AGE.  Only about 15 percent of female arrestees were under 18 years of age.  Overall, female offenders were somewhat younger than women in the general population.  While almost 63 percent of women in the general population were over 30, only about 43 percent of the female offenders were in this age group.

RACE.   While nearly two thirds of the women in the community were white, nearly two thirds of the arrested women were black.

OCCUPATION.   About two thirds of the female offenders were either unemployed or employed in unskilled jobs.  These women were more likely than women in the general population to be working but were also more likely to have unskilled jobs.

EDUCATION.  Over one third of the offenders had less than 9 years of education, compared with about one sixth of women in the general population.  Similarly, less than 10 percent of the offender group had more than 12 years of education.

MARITAL STATUS.  Female offenders were much less likely than women in the general population to be married.  Only about one third of the offender group were married, compared with more than 45 percent of women in the general population.

DEPENDENTS.  Arrested females were less likely to have dependent children under age 18.  More than half of the offenders, but more than 60 percent of women in the general population had dependent children.

Wolfe et al. went on to note how some of these characteristics are associated with patterns of crime. For example, females under 18 were most often involved in petty property offenses but had low rates for drug-alcohol offenses and sex crimes. Further, older women were most often involved in violent offenses, and in the use of alcohol and drugs. Unemployed women, even with high school degrees, were particularly likely to be arrested for sex offenses. White females dominated the alcohol-drug offenses but black females were over-represented for most other types of crime.

Thus, the image of the female offender that emerges from the Wolfe et al. study, supported by other more narrowly focused research, is of someone who is near the bottom of the socioeconomic ladder. She is likely to be under-educated and marginally employed at best. There is little in any of the literature to suggest that female offenders often engage in criminality to make a political or social statement. Instead, these women are often petty property offenders for whom crime is one method of "getting by."

## Explaining Female Criminality

Through the years, researchers have used a variety of approaches to explain female criminality. Some have focused on female criminality itself, while others have attempted to explain male/female differences in crime. For clarity of presentation these explanations will be divided into three categories, depending on whether they primarily focus on individual factors, small group processes, or the social structure.

### I. *Individual Factors*

Explanations of female criminality which focus on individual factors have tended to be a curious mixture of psychological and biological influences, in which personal pathology is cited as evidence of some biological deficiency or flaw. For example, Hahn (1980) reviewed 15 studies of cacogenic families published between 1875 and 1926 and concluded that women in these families were often portrayed as the primary initiators and transmitters of biological flaws directly associated with the criminality of these women and their family members. During this same introductory period, Lombroso and Ferrero (1916) published a study arguing that biological factors led to unusually sinister forms of criminality in women:

> We have seen that the normal woman is naturally less sensitive to pain than a man....We also saw that women have many traits in common with children; that their moral sense is deficient;

that they are revengeful, jealous, inclined to vengeances of a refined cruelty.

In ordinary cases these defects are neutralized by piety, maternity, want of passion, sexual coldness, by weakness and an underdeveloped intelligence. But when a morbid activity of the physical centers intensifies the bad qualities of women, and induces them to seek relief in evil deeds...it is clear that the innocuous semi-criminal present in the normal woman must be transformed into a born criminal more terrible than any man...the criminal woman is consequently a monster (pp. 150-152).

Lombroso and Ferrero also questioned the validity of the large sex differences observed in official statistics, suggesting that female criminality was more likely to be hidden and hence unrecorded.

Many of these biological arguments were restated by Pollak in 1950, whose relatively broad study of female criminality also included a consideration of social factors and of Freudian psychology. Pollak shared the view that females were as criminal as males and that female criminality was biologically based. He stressed the role of physical over-development (early maturation) as a precipitating factor in female criminality. Pollak also believed that the physical inferiority of women could not account for the relatively low rate of female crime, since technology now allows women to commit crimes requiring little physical strength—such as armed robbery.

Pollak added a Freudian tone to traditional biological explanations of female criminality, when he suggested that women were as criminal as men, but were less often caught because of their unusual powers of deceit. Pollak (1950) asserted that this superior ability to trick and deceive was related to the fact that women are born without a penis:

Man must achieve an erection in order to perform the sex act and will not be able to hide his failure...and pretense of sexual response is impossible for him, if it is lacking. Woman's body, however, permits such pretense to a certain degree and lack of orgasm does not prevent her ability to participate in the sex act. It cannot be denied that this basic physiological difference may well have a great influence on the degree of confidence which the two sexes have in the possible success of concealment and thus on their character pattern in this respect (p. 10).

Pollak also pointed to the influence of sexual mores requiring a woman to "conceal every four weeks the period of menstruation" (p. 10) and to conceal from her children the facts of life.

Shortly following the publication of Pollak's work, Satterfield (1953) reported a study of 20 delinquent and 20 nondelinquent females. He argued that female criminality arose from woman's inability to adequately learn the feminine role (e.g., housewife and mother) for which she was biologically destined. Satterfield believed that female delinquents were childlike and irresponsible and that biologically based sex differences in temperament accounted for male-female differences in crime.

More recently, Sparrow (1970), an attorney reporting on several sensational courtroom cases of murderesses, also focused on the capacity for evil innate to women:

> When it comes to preparation for the crime the natural aptitude of the woman for subterfuge and concealment stands her in good stead. She has always had to rely on a certain amount of convincing chicanery to make up for her lack of sheer physical strength (p. 8).

It can be seen that many of these explanations focus on hidden or as-yet-unspecified biological mechanisms within women. The existence of physiologically based "natural" or "innate" tendencies which motivate the female offender are assumed rather than demonstrated. Further, these studies tend to be based on unusual samples or on anecdotal incidents. Until these biological mechanisms can be more clearly specified and more rigorous scientific procedures applied to the research, such approaches are unlikely to yield much productive information about female criminality.

There are, however, several individualistic explanations which more clearly specify the biological factors to be examined. Generally, these explanations focus on the effects of either menstruation or testosterone levels. Dalton (1961) has focused on the link between crime and the stress experienced by women during menstruation. She found that nearly one-half of all crimes committed by a sample of inmates in a women's prison were committed during menstruation or in the premenstruum, and this association was particularly strong for first offenders. Dalton's conclusions have been sharply criticized by Horney (1978), who argued that menstruation may be induced by stressful events. For first offenders in particular, the process of arrest may be sufficiently stressful to induce menstruation, thus producing the high conjoint occurrence of menstruation and criminal behavior. Horney (1978) also noted that:

studies have failed to isolate a unitary pattern of symptoms experienced just before or during menstruation; rather, the reports of particular symptoms vary from one woman to the next. In fact, some of the reported symptoms appear to be direct opposites: e.g., constipation and diarrhea, insomnia and sleeping all day, fatigue and bursts of energy....The syndrome is not composed of symptoms uniquely associated with menstruation or even with women, but of symptoms often experienced by both sexes under stressful conditions (p. 26).

Horney argued that both the timing of the menstrual cycle and the nature of its accompanying symptoms are subject to social influence, so that it is premature to assume that menstruation directly causes criminal behavior.

The viability of menstruation as a facilitator of female criminality is still highly controversial. In 1981, Dalton's testimony was instrumental in the release of two British women, one charged with murder and the other, who had nearly 30 previous arrests, with attempted murder. Each successfully argued that their violent episodes were triggered by menstruation-induced stress ("British Legal Debate," 1981). In the U.S., however, defense attorneys dropped menstruation as a defense in a celebrated 1982 case because it seemed unlikely that it would succeed (Press & Clausen, 1982; Bird, 1982). It is unclear whether menstrual stress will eventually be accepted as a legitimate legal defense in the United States. In 1986, the American Psychiatric Association announced that premenstrual syndrome (PMS) would be added to the next addition of their official diagnostic manual as a recognized disorder (Boffey, 1986). Such professional recognition of PMS would ordinarily pave the way for its use as a defense in court. However, PMS was included in the appendix of the diagnostic manual, making its usefulness in the courts questionable.

Menstruation alone cannot explain why females have lower rates of crime than males, nor does it appear to account for much variance in female criminality. The study of menstruation may prove fruitful, however, when examined in combination with social and cultural influences which shape the individual's response to menstruation and to stress in general.

Finally, several authors have discussed the possible importance of testosterone as a biological basis for explaining the much lower crime rates for females compared with males. Gove (1985), for example, cites research which shows that high testosterone levels are related to aggression among adolescents, but not among adults. Since the effects of testosterone decline with age and since testosterone levels are lower in females, testosterone is offered by Gove as one possible explanation for the decline in criminality over time and for the lower rates of crime for females. As Bruinsma et al.

(1981) have noted, however, there are facts which cannot be accounted for by testosterone levels:

> Bearing in mind that testosterone production in women is relatively higher before puberty and after the climacterium than during the fertile years, one might expect increased "aggressive" behavior precisely during these two periods....On the contrary: female criminality is lowest during these two periods (p 47).

Further, as Sobel (1978) argues, the link between testosterone production and aggression is far from clear. It is just as likely, for example, that high levels of aggression may lead to the production of testosterone. Thus, although the focus on menstruation and on testosterone are positive beginnings in the search for relatively specific biological factors which account for female criminality, their importance has yet to be demonstrated.

The fact that female criminality remains persistently lower than male criminality across time and across a large number of cultures (as we will see in Chapter 2) makes biological arguments particularly appealing. Although the approach is intriguing, specific biological factors have not been identified which provide adequate explanations for female criminality. More importantly, there has been no clear articulation of the mechanisms by which *biological* factors influence *socially* defined behaviors. Despite the rather unimpressive contributions which have been made to date, these individualistic approaches promise to generate some of the most interesting and controversial research in the years ahead.

## II. *Small Group Processes*

There has been surprisingly little research on small group processes as they apply to female criminality. Part of the problem is that some female crimes (e.g., running away) are individualistic, creating the false impression that group processes simply don't apply to female criminals. As Erickson and Jensen (1977) have shown, however, females are just as likely as males to commit their delinquent acts in the company of peers. In fact, they found that for shoplifting, truancy, drinking, and marijuana use, females had higher group violation rates than males. Perhaps the major reason for the paucity of research is the striking absence of violent female gang activities. Both on the streets and in prisons female gangs are rare and nonviolent when compared with male gangs. As we will see in the discussion that follows, when female gangs have been identified, their character is often strikingly different from that of male gangs.

In the first and only large-scale study of its type, Frederick Thrasher's 1927 study of 1,313 Chicago gangs found little evidence of female gang activity:

> Gangs composed entirely of girls are exceedingly rare. Not more than five or six have been discovered in the present investigation. One of these was a group of colored girls in Chicago having baseball as their chief interest; another was organized for stealing; and the others were marginal cases, probably more really clubs than gangs (p.161).

Thrasher did note that girls were sometimes admitted as members to male gangs, but in these cases the girls took on masculine roles and if they chose to adopt feminine characteristics they could no longer maintain their role in the gang.

It was not until a 1963 magazine article by Robert Rice that female gangs were again recognized in the literature, but here again the contrast with male gangs is striking. Rice noted that although the females in his study identified themselves as members of a female gang, the Persian Queens, "none of the members, as far as I know, has a police record or is conspicuously delinquent in any way except sexually (1963:153)." Like Thrasher, Rice argued that these "gangs" were probably more appropriately described as clubs. Another feature of these gangs was the absence of regular group activity. Although the gang was small, the members seldom congregated and rarely undertook any activity as a group, except for weekly meetings at which attendance was sparse.

Fishman (1966) used reports from detached workers and personal observations to study a female gang, the Vice Queens, an auxiliary to a male gang, the Vice Kings. The Vice Queens oriented themselves toward male gang members and had few functions outside of their relationship to the male gang members. Like Rice, Fishman observed a loose and unstable structure of the female gang in comparison with that of the male gang. While members of the Vice Queens participated in group fighting, drinking, and other delinquency, such behavior was rare and played a small role in providing status. Status came, instead, from the male gang members and was centered on sexual activity.

In his study of the Molls, Miller (1973) also noted that status for female gang members derived from affiliation with a male gang. Most of the "crime" committed was of a petty nature and decidedly nonviolent. The Molls showed only about one-tenth the involvement in illegal activity of male gangs of the same socioeconomic status. Furthermore, neither their behaviors nor their attitudes reflected an adherence to the tenets of contemporary feminism.

Brown's 1977 discussion of black female gangs in Philadelphia argues that lower-class females join gangs for excitement and popularity. Females in these gangs were as likely to be involved in fighting as were male gangs, with one female gang having been accused of knifing and kicking pregnant females.

Giordano (1978) studied the group nature of delinquency among lower-class adolescent girls. Girls who were part of a regular group were more likely to be delinquent and were most likely to get into trouble when in mixed-sex groups. They did not appear to be simply following the wishes of delinquent boyfriends. In fact, the greatest percentage of delinquencies occurred in groups with more than one other male. In these mixed-sex peer groups, males were able to provide an appropriate body of knowledge of the techniques of delinquency. Over one half of the institutionalized females in the study indicated they had been part of a female "gang," and one-half of these said the gang had a name.

In a second study, Giordano and Cernkovich (1979) again observed that female criminality was most likely to occur in mixed-sex peer groups and that most girls thought they were less likely to get into trouble when in the company of just one male. In both delinquent and nondelinquent groups, girls who had close nonromantic male friends were also more delinquent, further supporting the view that males served as "educators" for females.

Bowker, Gross, and Klein (1980) reanalyzed interview data gathered in the 1960s from 207 Black youth, 40 percent of whom were affiliated with gangs. Of 182 reported delinquent acts, only 4 had been partially planned by girls. Furthermore, female delinquents were far more likely to be involved in acts with five or more others than in incidents with fewer participants. Delinquent boys were asked what would have happened had a female been involved in the act for which they were currently incarcerated. Sixty-eight percent  said the incident would have been postponed or canceled, 24 percent said the female would have been ignored, and 8 percent would have included the female in the delinquent act. Overall, these data suggested that females were rarely allowed access to the delinquent activities of the male gang and that the presence of females may have even suppressed delinquency by male gang members.

Bowker and Klein (1983) compared a sample of 122 gang and 100 non-gang girls matched for neighborhood, education, and age. All of the female gangs were affiliated with male gangs, and gang girls were similar to non-gang girls in terms of family structure, family socioeconomic status, self-image, or relations with mothers, fathers, or other adults. Relationships with *girlfriends* were the most important predictors of gang affiliation. Bowker and Klein concluded:

> ...personality variables have minimum relevance for gang membership and the number of offenses committed....the decision to join a gang or to participate in a serious delinquent act need not reflect personal maladjustment, excessive problems in relating to the opposite sex, or poor relations with parents (p 749-50).

The most recent and detailed study of female gangs was undertaken by Campbell (1984a, 1984b), who conducted a participant observation study of three New York City female gangs. Campbell notes that according to data from the New York City Police, females probably comprise no more than about ten percent of all gang members in the city and that half of New York gangs are Puerto Rican. Campbell spent six months each with: (1) Connie, leader of the Sandman Ladies, an auxiliary of a Puerto Rican male biker gang; (2) Weeza, leader of the Sex Girls, an auxiliary of a Puerto Rican male gang; and (3) Sun-Africa, member of The Five Percent Nation, a religious-cultural gang designed to teach young black males the correct ways of Islamic life. In each case, the woman was traditional in many ways. Connie and Weeza each had several children and had child care as their primary responsibility, and Sun-Africa was fully committed to serving the wishes of her male sponsor in the Five Percent Nation. None of the women were legally married, but all relied heavily on their relationships with male companions. The three lived in conditions of poverty in which violence was a common way of life. They all knew of close friends or other gang members who had been killed in fights or while committing crimes. The Sandman Ladies and the Sex Girls expected their members to be willing and able to fight for the honor of the gang. All three entered the gangs because of male companions, either brothers or boyfriends, who first exposed them to gang life and then persuaded them to become part of it. Unlike Bowker et al., (1980), Campbell's work suggests that females may often be instrumental in instigating fights between male gangs by making or receiving sexual advances from rival gang members. From Campbell's description, it appears that for each girl the gang served to provide some stability and harmony in their otherwise chaotic lives. Criminal activities and fighting sometimes went along with membership in the gang, but companionship and security always seemed to be the primary incentive for remaining in the gang.

Overall, the available data suggest that females are rarely members of gangs, and, when female gangs *are* formed, they tend to serve as auxiliaries to male gangs. Female gangs are nonviolent compared with their male counterparts and appear to be of a relatively transient nature. Further, there is little evidence of a growing problem of female gang activity. Two of the three gangs studied by Campbell (1984a), for example, were in decline and had only a few members left.

## III. *Social Structure*

The most prolific and heated arguments surrounding female criminality have focused on larger structural issues. Most of this research has focused on the "convergence hypothesis," which assumes that "as the social roles of the sexes are equalized, the differences between the sexes in terms of crime rates is diminished (Nettler, 1978, p. 124)." As we have argued above, however, little "convergence" of male and female criminality seems to have taken place. Nevertheless, the *belief* that such convergence has taken place has led to a large body of research. Further, we are faced with the even more interesting dilemma of explaining why, if women's roles have become more egalitarian over time, their criminality has not followed suit.

From the assumption of convergence, two dominant strands of explanation for female criminality have arisen. The first is that male and female crime rates differ because of structurally blocked opportunities, and the second is that differences arise from socialization practices and differing sex-role orientations.

Opportunity theory assumes that crime is linked directly to one's position in the occupational structure. Female criminality is less frequent than male criminality because females are less likely to be in the labor force or in positions of trust that allow for the commission of such crimes as fraud or embezzlement. Simon (1975), for example, has argued that female criminality has been on the increase, but only for property crimes (larceny, fraud, embezzlement, etc.) rather than for violent crimes such as homicide or robbery. She reasoned that the disproportionate increase in property crime was the result of more women entering the labor market and finding themselves in positions that permitted the commission of such offenses.

Although initially popular, the opportunity hypothesis has not generated strong empirical support. Noblit and Burkhart (1976) found that crimes by the young and crimes of violence increased at a greater rate than would be predicted by the opportunity hypothesis. Examining both self-report and official data, Weis (1976) concluded that there was stronger support for the opportunity hypothesis than for its alternatives, although the data were more suggestive than conclusive. Steffensmeier (1980) argued that even though there were increases in property offenses by females, these increases had begun prior to the late 1960s and early 1970s when the women's movement should have had its greatest impact on changing occupational roles.   Steffensmeier suggested that even if occupational roles had been changing, factors such as institutionalized sexism may have been more significant in maintaining relatively stable levels of female criminality.

Taking a unique approach to examining the opportunity hypothesis, Bartel (1979) tested an economic model of female criminality and concluded that increases were not the result of greater labor force participation.   Increases were less related to changes from female to male work-role orientation than to changes within the female's *family* role. There was an inverse relationship between the average number of preschool children in husband-wife families and criminal activity by married males. Over one-half of the increase in female criminality between 1960 and 1970 could be accounted for by decreases in the average number of preschool children in the family.   These findings suggest that changes in the domestic role may be more significant than changes in work roles outside the home in accounting for increases in female criminality.

Some have suggested that female criminality can better be explained by differing role orientations of males and females.   As women adopt increasingly masculine roles and identities, they will approach males in both the quantity and quality of criminal activity.   Thus, it is suggested that female delinquents will have a more "masculine orientation" than female nondelinquents and that both property and violent offenses will increase as sex roles converge (Adler, 1975).

Research on the impact of social role orientation has yielded inconclusive results.   Shover, Norland, James, and Thornton (1979) and Thornton and James (1979) found no association between masculine orientation and female delinquency.   Norland, Wessel, and Shover (1981) also found that among females, the effects of masculine orientation were small, indirect, and opposite the predicted direction.   A study by Cullen, Golden, and Cullen (1979) reported a positive relationship between masculinity and delinquency, although delinquency by males was more influenced than was delinquency by females.   In addition, Cullen et al. noted a persistent sex difference beyond that attributable to masculine orientation, suggesting that additional influences were at work.   In a 1979 study, Giordano and Cernkovich argued that sex roles must be treated as multidimensional.   They found that a liberated attitude toward work and family was not associated with female delinquency, but attitude toward appropriate behavior for females was associated with delinquent behavior. Finally, Bainbridge and Crutchfield (1983), finding no link between sex role ideology and delinquency among either males or females, argued that sex role is a "complex cluster of cultural facts" which has no simple relationship to crime.

While a variety of studies have examined the link between masculinity and delinquency, the results of these studies suggest that masculinity is of only limited usefulness in explaining female delinquency or sex differences in delinquency. Naffin (1985) argues that this body of research has been flawed by relying on concepts (masculinity and femininity) which are so vague and imprecise that they are of little value for empirical research. A female rated as "masculine" by one scale, for example, might be found "feminine" or "androgynous" by another. Thus, the way in which masculinity or femininity are operationally defined significantly influences the conclusions reached. Further, social scientists have been unable to reach any agreement about the nature of masculinity and femininity and thus cannot explain *why* or *how* they should be related to criminality. Until these fundamental problems are resolved, it seems unlikely that studies of masculinity/femininity and crime will ever prove fruitful in advancing our understanding of female criminality.

Some of the most promising structural-level ideas about female criminality have been developed in two studies by John Hagan and his associates. In a 1979 study, Hagan, Simpson, and Gillis argued that female criminality was related to the fact that women had more restricted access than men to the reward structure of the social stratification system. This was not simply a matter of overt economic discrimination or exclusion, as Simon (1975) had argued, but was also a function of men more generally being assigned to the public arena, and women to the private sphere (e.g., the home). Thus, the sexual stratification of crime was linked ultimately to the stratification of work. As national and international markets developed, work came increasingly to take place outside the home for men only. Women were entering the labor force at a much slower rate than males; thus, males came more and more to work in public places: "The result was to subject men increasingly to the formal social control of an emerging criminal justice system, while leaving women to the informal social control of the family (Hagan et al., 1979, p. 26)." Their model was supported in their study of male and female high school students in which it was found that:

> ...although both mothers *and* fathers control their daughters more than their sons, mothers control their daughters even more than their fathers do....Thus, we have argued that in the world of crime and delinquency, as in the world of work, women are denied full access to the public sphere through a socialization sequence that moves from mother to daughter in a

cycle that is self-renewing....It is our hypothesis that peer groups, and later work groups, help to extend patterns established in childhood socialization....many female peer groups probably still reinforce dependence, compliance and passivity among their members (1979, p. 33-35).

The ideas first put forth in this 1979 study were expanded and refined in a more recent work (Hagan et al., 1985) in which they not only considered the *authority* exerted in the family setting, but the *power* available to the youth as reflected in the occupational/social class position of the family. This study again shows that females are more extensively controlled in the family setting and that youth from the upper classes are less likely to feel threatened by the risk of punishment. "The core assumption of our theory is that the presence of power and the absence of control create conditions of freedom that permit common forms of delinquency (1985, p. 1174)." Although their theory was not designed to explain serious delinquency, it is one of the few explanations for sex differences in crime which is based on a broad theoretical framework, is empirically verifiable, and is consistent with a large body of existing data regarding female criminality.

## Summary

From the mid-1970s on, there has been a growing interest in female offenders and their criminal behavior. For a while some argued that female criminality was increasing at a dramatic rate, and that these changes were particularly marked for violent crime. Although the popular press may have increased its coverage of female criminality, arrest statistics from the FBI suggest that violent crime by women has increased little compared with that of males. Further, there is little evidence to suggest that male and female rates for either violent or property crime are converging. Crime in America was and continues to be a predominantly male activity. Any changes in the structure of our society brought about by women's liberation or the increased participation of women in the labor force have not been of sufficient magnitude to generate a dramatic increase in female criminality or a "new breed" of female offender. FBI statistics make it clear that the crimes for which women are most often arrested are minor offenses, such as writing bad checks or shoplifting.

The absence of dramatic shifts in female criminality does not diminish the importance of studying the female offender. She is of interest *precisely because* her offending is relatively minor and infrequent. Understanding why female criminality differs so dramatically from that of males may tell us a great deal about the nature of all crime. While female criminality has been studied from a variety of perspectives, none has proven completely satisfactory. Biological explanations are intriguing but are still too rudimentary. For example, they have not addressed the mechanisms by which a *biological* factor such as testosterone might produce a *social* action such as shoplifting. Further, even when focusing on aggressive crimes, studies based on testosterone or the premenstrual syndrome have not been able to determine the extent to which these factors are *causes* or *effects* of aggressive criminality. Small group studies focusing on females and gang behavior are interesting, but so little work has been done in this area that theoretical explanations have not yet surfaced. Finally, those focusing on the social structure have approached female criminality from several perspectives. The evidence is weak at best for those who argue that "masculinity" or "femininity" are related to delinquency or adult crime. Conceptual and measurement issues raise serious questions about the possibility of explaining crime by examining sex-role orientation. A more fruitful approach has been that taken by John Hagan and his associates who have focused on the differences between men and women in the way they are regulated or controlled in our society.

Overall, the study of female criminality has the potential for dramatically improving our understanding of crime in general. Just as importantly, the study of female criminality tells us a great deal about the noncriminal roles occupied by men and women in our society.

# References

Adler, F. (1975). *Sisters in crime.* New York: McGraw-Hill.

Bainbridge, W.S., & Crutchfield, R.D. (1983). Sex role ideology and delinquency. *Sociological Perspectives, 26*(3), 253-274.

Bartel, A.P. (1979). Women and crime: An economic analysis. *Economic Inquiry, 17*(1), 29-51.

Bird, D. (1982, November 4). Defense linked to menstruation dropped in case. *New York Times,* p. B4.

Boffey, P.M. (1986, July 2). 3 new psychiatric categories are accepted. *New York Times,* p. 11.

Bonger, W. (1916). *Crime and economic conditions.* Boston: Little, Brown.

Bowker, L.H., Gross, H.S., & Klein, M.W. (1980). Female participation in delinquent gang activities. *Adolescence, 15*(59), 509-519.

Bowker, L.H., & Klein, M.W. (1983). The etiology of female juvenile delinquency and gang membership: A test of psychological and social structural explanations. *Adolescence, 18*(72):739-751.

British legal debate: Premenstrual tension and criminal behavior (1981, December 29). *New York Times,* p. C3.

Brown, W.K. (1977). Black female gangs in Philadelphia. *International Journal of Offender Therapy and Comparative Criminology, 21*(3), 221-228.

Bruinsma, G.J.N., Dessaur, C.I., & Van Hezewijk, W.J.V. (1981). In F. Adler (Ed.), *The incidence of female criminality in the contemporary world.* New York: New York University Press.

Campbell, A. (1984a). *The Girls in the Gang.* New York: Basil Blackwell.

Campbell, A. (1984b). Girls' talk: The social representation of aggression by female gang members. *Criminal Justice and Behavior, 11*(2), 139-156.

Canter, R.J. (1982).  Sex differences in self-report delinquency. *Criminology 20*(2), 373-393.

Cullen, F.T., Golden, K.M., & Cullen, J.B. (1979).  Sex and delinquency: A partial test of the masculinity hypothesis. *Criminology, 17*(3), 301-310.

Dalton, K. (1961).   Menstruation and crime. *British Medical Journal,* December 30, 1752-1753.

Erickson, M.L. & Jensen, G.F. (1977).   "Delinquency is still group behavior!": Toward revitalizing the group premise in the sociology of deviance. *Journal of Criminal Law and Criminology, 68*(2):262-273.

Fishman, L.T. (1966).  *Aspirations and delinquency: The case of Negro girls.* Unpublished master's thesis, University of Chicago.

Giordano, P.C. (1978).  Girls, guys and gangs: The changing social context of female delinquency. *Journal of Criminal Law and Criminology, 68*(1), 126-132.

Giordano, P.C., & Cernkovich, S.A. (1979).   On complicating the relationship between liberation and delinquency. *Social Problems, 26*(4), 467-481.

Gove, W. (1985).   The effect of age and gender on deviant behavior: A biopsychosocial perspective. In A. S. Rossi (Ed.), *Gender and the Life Course.* (pp. 115-144). New York: Aldine.

Hagan, J. (1985).   Toward a structural theory of crime, race, and gender: The Canadian case. *Crime and Delinquency, 31*(1), 129-146.

Hagan, J., Gillis, A.R., & Simpson, J. (1985).   The class structure of gender and delinquency: Toward a power-control theory of common delinquent behavior. *American Journal of Sociology, 90*(6), 1151-1178.

Hagan, J., Simpson, J.H., & Gillis, A.R. (1979).   The sexual stratification of social control: A gender-based perspective on crime and delinquency. *British Journal of Sociology, 30*(1), 25-38.

Hahn, N.F. (1980).   Too dumb to know better: Cacogenic family studies and the criminology of women. *Criminology 18*(1), 3-25.

Hindelang, M.J. (1971).   Age, sex, and the versatility of delinquent involvements. *Social Problems, 18*(4), 522-535.

Horney, J. (1978).   Menstrual cycles and criminal responsibility. *Law and Human Behavior, 2*(1), 25-36.

Lombroso, C., & Ferrero, G. (1916).   *The female offender.* New York: Appleton.

Mawby, R. (1980).   Sex and crime: The results of a self-report study. *British Journal of Sociology, 31*(4), 525-543.

Miller, W.B. (1973).   The Molls. *Society, 11*(1), 32-35.

Naffin, N. (1985).   The masculinity-femininity hypothesis: A consideration of gender-based personality theories of female crime. *British Journal of Criminology, 25*(4), 365-381.

Nash, J.R. (1981).   *Look for the Woman.* New York: M. Evans and Co.

Nettler, G. (1978).   *Explaining Crime.* (2nd ed.). New York: McGraw-Hill.

Noblit, G.W., & Burkhart, J.M. (1976).   Women and crime: 1960-1970. *Social Science Quarterly, 56*(4), 650-657.

Norland, S., Wessel, R.C., & Shover, N. (1981).   Masculinity and delinquency. *Criminology, 19*(3), 421-433.

O'Brien, R.M. (1985).   *Crime and victimization data.* Beverly Hills: Sage.

Pollak, O. (1950).   *The criminality of women.* Westport, CT: Greenwood Press.

Press, A., & Clausen, P. (1982, November 8).   Not guilty because of PMS? *Newsweek.* p. 111.

Rice, R. (1963, October 19). The Persian Queens. *The New Yorker,* pp. 153-187.

Richards, P. (1981).   Quantitative and qualitative sex differences in middle-class delinquency. *Criminology, 18*(4), 453-470.

Satterfield, V.B. (1953). Criminal responsibility of women. *Journal of Criminal Law, Criminology, and Police Science, 43*(6), 756-763.

Schur, E.M., & Bedau, H.A. (1974). *Victimless crimes: Two sides of a controversy.* Englewood Cliffs, NJ: Prentice-Hall.

Shover, N., Norland, S., James, J., & Thornton, W.E. (1979). Gender roles and delinquency. *Social Forces, 58*(1), 162-175.

Simon, R.J. (1975). *The contemporary woman and crime.* Washington, DC: U.S. Government Printing Office.

Smart, C. (1979). The new female criminality: Reality or myth? *British Journal of Criminology, 19*(1), 50-59.

Sobel, E. (1978). The aggressive female. In I.L. Kutash, S.B. Kutash, L.B. Schlesinger, & Associates. (Eds.), *Violence: perspectives on murder and aggression.* San Francisco: Jossey-Bass.

Schlesinger, B. & Associates (Eds.), *Violence: Perspectives on Murder and Aggression.* San Francisco: Jossey-Bass.

Sparrow, G. (1970). *Women who murder.* London: Arthur Barker Limited.

Spierling, F. (1984). *Lizzie.* New York: Random House.

Steffensmeier, D.J. (1978). Crime and the contemporary woman: An analysis of changing levels of female property crime, 1960-75. *Social Forces* 57(2), 566-84.

Steffensmeier, D.J. (1980). Sex differences in patterns of adult crime, 1965-1977: A review and assessment. *Social Forces, 58*(3), 1080-1108.

Thornton, W.E., & James, J. (1979). Masculinity and delinquency revisited. *British Journal of Criminology, 19*(3), 225-241.

Thrasher, F.M. (1963). *The Gang.* Chicago: University of Chicago Press.

U.S. Bureau of the Census (1965-84). *Current population reports, series P-25.* Washington, DC: U.S. Government Printing Office.

U.S. Department of Justice, Federal Bureau of Investigation (1965-84). *Uniform crime reports*. Washington, DC: U.S. Government Printing Office.

Weis, J.G. (1976). Liberation and crime: The invention of the new female criminal. *Crime and Social Justice, 6*(Fall-Winter), 17-27.

Wolfe, N.T., Cullen, F.T., & Cullen, J.B. (1984). Describing the female offender: A note on the demographics of arrests. *Journal of Criminal Justice, 12*(5), 438-492.

# 2

# Comparative Studies

## Introduction

American women have no monopoly on crime. Some of the most colorful and visible criminals in other countries have also been women. For example:

MATA HARI. Margaret MacLeod, or Mata Hari, may be among the most famous spies in history. At age 19 she married a man more than twice her age, who was abusive and led her into prostitution. Following her divorce, she engaged in prostitution and exotic dancing, for which she gained fame throughout Europe. Adopting the name Mata Hari and pretending to come from the East Indies, she danced for and socialized with nobility from several European countries. Through her relationship with Berlin's Chief of Police, Mata Hari spied for the Germans during World War I. The French, believing that her information may have led to the deaths of more than 200,000 French soldiers, had her arrested and tried for espionage. She was found guilty and executed by a French firing squad in 1917 (Nash, 1981).

MAY ELIAS MANSOUR. In April of 1986 a bomb was set off aboard an airliner shortly after it left the airport in Athens, killing four passengers and injuring nine others. Though her involvement was never proven, police suspected that the bombing was the work of May Elias Mansour, who was also reputed to have been involved in other airline bombings. Ms. Mansour is described by the police as a "known terrorist" who was also involved in attacks on Israelis during Israel's 1982 invasion of Lebanon.   (Mansour Surfaces to Deny Bomb Charges, 1986).

JENNY DIVER.   Jenny Diver may be the most famous pickpocket and swindler in the history of England.   Churches, public celebrations, and special events were attended by Jenny and her accomplices whose techniques were often ingenious.  In one scheme, for example, she created an elaborate gown with false arms and hands which would rest on her lap while her real arms reached into the pockets of churchgoers.  In 1740, at the age of 40, she was caught pickpocketing for a second time and was hanged (Nash, 1981).

FUSAKO SHIGENOBU.  Leader of the Japanese Red Army, a left-wing extremist group, Fusako Shigenobu was instrumental in airline hijackings, the occupation of embassies and a number of bombings.   In 1977 the group made headlines when the Japanese government agreed to pay a six million dollar ransom demand and release 9 extremists from prison in exchange for the lives of 146 passengers aboard a hijacked Japan Air Lines DC-8.  Her husband had been killed in a 1972 attack on the Tel Aviv airport and her brother-in-law was among the prisoners released by the government (Malcolm, 1977).

It is clear from the discussion in Chapter 1 that even if the women's liberation movement in the United States has had a major impact on the lifestyles of women, it has not had much influence on their criminality. These findings, however, do not lessen the importance of studying female criminality, for even if it has changed little, discovering why it is so infrequent relative to men is an important research question. Furthermore, discounting the influence of women's liberation does not allow us to discount the importance of male and female roles in accounting for differences in the nature and extent of their criminality.  The relative stability of American society makes it difficult to answer the question of whether dramatically different female roles would result in dramatically different forms of female criminality.  Some have argued, for example, that women's liberation is largely a myth and that women's roles have changed little over the past few decades (Hewlett, 1986).  Another way to consider the importance of male and female roles for criminal behavior is to look beyond the cultural boundaries of the United States to examine the social roles and criminality of women in different cultural settings.

Although much of the existing literature on female criminality focuses on the American situation, it would be a mistake to believe that female criminality is a uniquely American problem. In fact, the United States includes less than five percent of the world's population and only a few of the hundreds of cultures of the world (cf. Lee, 1984). Similarly, there is no reason why the *form* of female criminality in the U.S. must be identical to that throughout the world. Consider, for example, the greater role played by women in the commission of politically motivated violence in several European and Middle-Eastern countries.

Much of the research on female criminality has been based on data from the U.S. and Great Britain. Unfortunately, published studies of female criminality in other countries are less readily available. This chapter will summarize much of what we know about female criminality around the world and will illustrate how cultural variations may not only provide a better understanding of female criminality, but of crime in general. While studying female criminality in a variety of cultural settings may improve our understanding of the problem, it is essential to recognize that the comparative approach also has serious limitations.

## Issues in Cross-Cultural Research

A logical first step in making comparisons of female criminality among various countries is to use official crime data. Unfortunately, it is simply not possible to make direct comparisons with these data. There are at least four reasons why such comparisons are problematic.

First, many countries do not collect or report their crime data. For example, in her collection of original articles on female criminality throughout the world, Adler (1981:10) noted:

> Hardest to tell is the story of the African experience. Most of the countries of this continent emerged from colonial domination only a few years ago, and Africans are preoccupied with tasks of nation building, food production, education, and the eradication of diseases, so that problems of establishing crime statistics or of fighting crime takes second billing.

In other countries, such as the Soviet Union, crime statistics are collected but are considered a state secret.

A second problem is that studying crime statistics over time requires a relatively stable government, or at least the existence of stable government agencies to collect data. We might expect that countries which undergo major social upheavals might also see the most dramatic changes in female criminality, but these are precisely the countries *least* likely to maintain records over time.

A third problem is that countries are likely to vary tremendously in the way in which crimes are defined, making comparisons of one country with another problematic. For example, in most cultures females are more likely than males to carry out infanticide, but there are considerable cultural variations in the extent to which infanticide is defined as murder, a unique offense, or no offense at all (cf. Das, 1960). Further, even when infanticide is *legally* defined as a crime, it may be socially tolerated (particularly for infant females) and hence seldom enter official statistics (e.g. Chang, 1982). This also illustrates how the problem of comparing crime statistics from different cultures goes beyond simple problems of legal definitions and includes the social context in which those laws are enforced. For example, even if two countries have the same legal definition and the same actual occurrence of infanticide, their official rates may be vastly different if infanticide offenders in one society are seldom reported to the police.

A fourth problem is peculiar to the study of female criminality. There are likely to be differences from one culture to the next in the willingness of victims to report female offenders to the police. For example, while Hindelang (1979) found that in the U.S. victims had few hesitations about reporting female offenders, Bhanot and Misra (1981) report that in India there are strong social pressures against bringing female offenders to the attention of authorities.

Taken together, these four problems raise serious questions about the wisdom of using official statistics to compare female criminality across countries. Generally, researchers have taken one of two approaches in response to these problems. First, when comparing several countries, only the broadest categories of crime are used, rather than comparing specific offenses. It is assumed that this partially alleviates the problem of variations in the definition of crime in that any underrepresentation of women because of the way a crime is defined in one country will be offset by the underrepresentation of another crime category in another country. The assumption that such equal and opposite biasing influences will yield figures which will be directly comparable is highly suspect and has never been tested. A second approach is to forego any large-scale comparison *among* countries and focus on case studies of specific nations. This approach has the advantage of providing a better understanding of the social context in which female criminality takes place in any one country. The disadvantage of numerous case studies, however, is that it is difficult to make comparisons among countries if there is no standardized procedure for data collection.

Our attention now turns to studies utilizing each of these approaches. First, we will examine those studies which compare a relatively large number of countries simultaneously.   Next, we will discuss several of the more interesting case studies which have examined female crime outside of the United States.

## Utilizing International Crime Data

At present there is only one source of world-wide criminal statistics. Since 1950, the International Criminal Police Organization (INTERPOL) has sent standard forms to member countries throughout the world.  These forms include information about the total population of the country, crime rates, and the percent of offenses committed by females, by juveniles, and by aliens.  In addition, (for 1981-82) crimes are broken into the following 13 categories:  murder, sex offenses (including rape), rape, serious assault, theft (all kinds), aggravated theft, robbery and violent theft, breaking and entering, theft of motor cars, other thefts, fraud, counterfeit currency offenses, and drug offenses.  Response to the forms is voluntary, so that the countries included in one report may not be included in others and participating countries vary from one report to the next.  Further, many countries do not break down their criminal statistics by sex or age.  In fact, consistent annual reporting of crime by sex of the offender is the exception rather than the rule.

Sensitive to problems with the data and to potential misuses of the data, the 1981-1982 report also includes the following warning:

> The information given is in no way intended for use as a basis for comparisons between different countries.  Our statistics cannot take account of the differences that exist between the legal definitions of punishable offenses in various countries, of the different methods of calculation, or of any changes which may have occurred in the countries concerned during the reference period.  All of these factors obviously have repercussions on the figures supplied....Consequently, the figures given in these statistics must be interpreted with caution.

To illustrate the extent to which non-reporting is a problem with INTERPOL data, reports were assembled for the following eleven years: 1950-52, 1961-62, 1971-72, 1975-76, and 1981-82.  Over these eleven years, 110 countries reported data at one time or another, but of these, only eight reported crime data for each year and only Germany and Monaco reported the percent of female offenders each year.  In fact, one-third of the countries reported crime data for only one or two of the eleven years and about half reported breakdowns of crime by sex for fewer than three of the eleven years.  Thus, even if we were to accept INTERPOL data as a valid measure of female criminality, examining trends over time is problematic given the amount of missing data.

Thus, researchers are in the position of being unable to make direct comparisons across countries with the only long-term international crime data available.  Given these constraints it should not be surprising that few comparative studies of female criminality have been conducted.  There are, however, several studies which have made interesting use of INTERPOL data.

In a brief appendix to her groundbreaking study *The Contemporary Woman and Crime*, Rita Simon presented one of the first efforts to utilize INTERPOL data to examine female criminality on an international scale.  Though her discussion was brief and her use of the data cautious, she concluded there was little relationship between the amount of female crime and the level of economic development.  Using data from 24 countries for 1963, 1968 and 1970, she found only a few in which there was a trend toward higher arrest rates for women.  "And those countries in which there was a trend could not be characterized as homogeneous by their predominant economic or social characteristics (1975:94)."  Next, she ranked these countries according to the proportion of female offenders to determine if countries with high rates were similar in their culture or economic development.  She found that:

> The countries that have the highest female arrest rates for all crimes are a mixed lot of modern and traditional, Western and Eastern, industrial/technological and agrarian.  They include Thailand, the West Indies, and Tunisia, together with Germany, England, and France.  Among those countries there is considerable variation in women's roles and their status(1975:94).

The next study to examine female criminality in a world perspective was conducted by Freda Adler in 1977.  Utilizing data from INTERPOL, as well as special crime reports published by individual nations, Adler was interested in testing her thesis that changing female roles would relate to increases in female criminality.  She generally concluded that as economic disparity between the sexes was reduced male and female crime rates converged, but this conclusion had several important qualifications.  First, Adler focused almost entirely on *percentage change* in the rate of female criminality. As discussed in Chapter 1, however, percentage change can be quite misleading when examining crime trends. Further, while increases in female criminality were larger than for males in most countries, nearly everywhere females constituted a small proportion of offenders—usually less than 15 percent, and most of these were minor nonviolent offenses. Even where changes appeared to have taken place females trailed far behind males in their criminality. Second, Adler assumed changing female roles in most nations but did not present any measures of these changes. Thus, most of her conclusions about changing female roles were impressionistic, rather than based on any actual measurement of female roles. Finally, the very nature of the data, that is national figures, made it difficult to determine the extent to which any changes in female criminality were a response to changing female roles. Male police officers and judges, for example, might have changed the way they treated women as their legal systems became more formal and bureaucratic. This would be an influence quite apart from actual increases in female criminality resulting from the emancipation of women, but would also lead to an increase in official criminality by females.

Despite these criticisms, it is important to recognize the landmark nature of both Adler's and Simon's work. They were among the first to recognize the importance of taking a world perspective on female criminality. Their approach was thought-provoking and has shaped the work of others who have since recognized the importance of the issues they raised.

In his 1978 book on women and crime, Bowker devoted a chapter to a discussion of international issues in female criminality. Examining INTERPOL reports for 1950, 1955, 1960, 1965, and 1972, he found only 30 countries which reported data on female criminality for at least two years which were also a minimum of one decade apart. Contrary to what Adler had predicted, Bowker found that female murder was declining rather than increasing worldwide. Further, for crime in general, he noted that: "The consistency in proportionate female crime over the years is much more significant than the changes that are found (1978:265)." To further explore the issue, Bowker looked at the link between female criminality and (1) educational equality between the sexes, (2) economic equality, and (3) national socioeconomic development. Overall crime was related only to socioeconomic development, leading him to conclude that in modernized nations females represent a greater proportion of criminal offenders. Finally, Bowker (1978) examined the imprisonment of females in Canada, India, Denmark, Australia, and New Zealand, noting that all of these countries incarcerated about the same proportion of females (between 2 and 5 percent of inmates are women).

Bowker concluded there was little support for Adler's (1977) assertion that throughout the world female criminality was undergoing a revolution, becoming more and more similar to male criminality in form and frequency. Many of the observed changes were either of a minor nature or followed no clear pattern.

Shortly after the work of Adler and of Bowker, Simon and Sharma (1979) also utilized INTERPOL data to examine world trends in female criminality.   They noted that between 1963 and 1972 there was no consistent pattern of change in overall rates or for specific offenses by females, although acts involving larceny did show a consistently upward trend among the more industrialized countries.   Simon and Sharma then examined changing crime patterns for three specific countries: the United States, Japan, and Israel. Japan was selected because it was a non-Western culture while Israel was selected because it shares many common features with U.S. culture.   Further, both Japan and Israel underwent profound changes in their societies following World War II and neither country has seen the development of a strong women's movement like that in the U.S. Only in the United States did the arrest rate of females for all crimes go up. In Israel the pattern was cyclical while in Japan the female arrest rate actually went down between 1963 and 1972. They also "found no evidence in any of the three societies that females were increasing their participation in violent offenses (1979:398)." Simon and Sharma next considered the influence of changing female labor force participation on female criminality. In Israel the upward trend was small while in Japan there was a decrease in the proportion of women in the labor force. Only in the U.S. was there a large increase in female labor force participation over time, and only in the U.S. were changes in female labor force participation directly associated with changes in female criminality.  In both Israel and Japan female labor force participation was negatively related to female criminality.  That is, when female labor force participation increased in Israel and Japan, their rate of female criminality actually declined, though not in a consistent pattern.

Marshall (1982) was interested in comparing Adler's argument that emancipation led to violent crime with Simon's thesis that emancipation leads to property crime through increased opportunities.   She used INTERPOL data for 1963-1970 from 14 developed nations.  Ironically, the two countries with the highest proportion of female arrests had relatively low proportions of economically active females, and the three countries with the lowest female criminality had relatively high levels of economic involvement by females.   Overall, she found little support for Adler's hypothesis, but Simon's opportunity theory was partially supported, in that female participation in the work force was related to the rate of arrest for fraud.

Hartnagel (1982) used 1971 INTERPOL data for 40 countries across four broad categories of crime: homicide, larceny, theft, and fraud. He was interested in determining if modernization and other characteristics of societies were associated with female criminality. In particular, he considered the country's gross national product, the extent to which it was urbanized, female political participation (years since universal suffrage), the domestic role participation of women (marriage and fertility rate), economic involvement (labor force participation, proportion of females among the economically active population, and segregation by occupation), and female education level. Overall, Hartnagel found little support for the hypothesis that modernity of the country or social participation by women were associated with female criminality. What associations were observed were for property offenses and were relatively minor. Hartnagel found that:

> Contrary to our expectations, female social-role participation had no appreciable effect on female crime rates. This would appear to suggest that the distinction between female domestic- and public-role participation is not of particular importance in explaining cross-national variation in female crime. Furthermore, it may be that modernization fails to change in any fundamental way the social status of women (1982:488).

Finally, Wilson (1983) summarized many of the previous studies, noting that when examined in a world perspective there is little evidence to support the contention that as women become more equal with men their crime rates become more similar. Further, she notes that while much has been written about the changing nature of female crime, there is little evidence to support such arguments. Most interesting is her comparison of three studies, all of which were based on INTERPOL data. There were numerous countries in which the *interpretation* of the trend in female criminality differed from one author to the next. The trend in female criminality in Finland, for example, was described by one author as upward, by another as downward, and by yet another as erratic. These kinds of differences illustrate the difficulty of making sense of the world picture of female criminality. The "facts" about female criminality are by no means clear-cut and are based on data of questionable quality. In addition to bringing our attention to the problems of interpreting world crime data, Wilson reminds us that such things as "liberation" and "equality" of the sexes may be thought of and measured in a variety of ways. Women's emancipation, for example, may be defined as: (1) an organized political-social movement; (2) a social-psychological state, such as the consciousness of women about their status; or (3) structural-economic, such as labor force participation by women.  Determining whether women's emancipation is related to female criminality becomes nearly impossible if there is no agreement about the meaning of emancipation which, in turn, influences the means by which it is measured.

TABLE 2.1

Percentage of Women Among All Arrests for All Crimes
in Selected Countries for 1963, 1968, 1970, and 1981.

| Country | 1963 | 1968 | 1970 | 1981 | Aver. | Trend |
|---|---|---|---|---|---|---|
| New Zealand | 8.2 | 11.9 | 41.0 | 15.9 | 19.3 | UP |
| Germany | 15.6 | 16.1 | 17.2 | 19.4 | 17.1 | UP |
| Portugal | 16.9 | 17.6 | 16.9 | 16.5 | 17.0 | NONE |
| Austria | 14.3 | 13.6 | 13.6 | 16.2 | 14.4 | NONE |
| Israel | 11.4 | 13.6 | 11.1 | 12.9 | 12.3 | NONE |
| Ireland | 12.1 | 9.6 | 9.0 | 14.9 | 11.4 | NONE |
| Korea | 9.2 | 12.6 | 10.9 | 8.8 | 10.4 | NONE |
| Burma | 12.0 | 5.8 | 15.7 | 7.2 | 10.2 | NONE |
| Netherlands | 10.9 | 10.4 | 10.1 | 7.8 | 9.8 | DOWN |
| Japan | 2.8 | 8.5 | 2.5 | 18.2 | 8.0 | NONE |
| Monaco | 5.9 | 5.7 | 10.5 | 9.5 | 7.9 | UP |
| Finland | 7.0 | 6.6 | 6.3 | 8.8 | 7.2 | NONE |
| Malawi | 4.8 | 3.5 | 4.5 | 6.4 | 4.8 | NONE |
| Hong Kong | 3.4 | 2.6 | 2.7 | 8.7 | 4.4 | NONE |

Source: Data for 1963, 1968, 1970 and 1981 from International Criminal Police Organization (INTERPOL).  International Crime Statistics.  Paris: INTERPOL.

Before closing this section, we wish to provide a brief update on Simon's initial work by adding 1981 crime figures to those she presented for 1963, 1968, and 1970. This will give the reader a more current picture of the international scene, since none of the studies cited here used INTERPOL data more recent than 1972.

Several things about Table 2.1 are worth noting. First, in only three countries (New Zealand, Germany, and Monaco) does female criminality follow an upward trend, and only in the Netherlands does it appear to be going down. For the remaining 11 countries, no persistent pattern can be detected. These data also show the dramatic shifts which may occur from one reporting period to the next, such as in New Zealand where females went from 8, to 12, to 41, to 16 percent of offenders during the course of the four reporting periods. It is impossible to determine the extent to which such fluctuations represent actual changes in female criminality or are simply artifacts of reporting procedures, but such shifts do raise serious questions about the quality of data provided by these reports. Another point about Table 2.1 is that only 14 countries provided data on female criminality for each of these time periods, with the notable absence of such countries as the United States, Great Britain, Canada, Mexico, France, and Italy.

Despite some disagreements about world crime patterns, and serious questions about the data used to make these comparisons, there are several consistent findings from the research summarized above. First, in all countries female criminality, except for special crimes like prostitution, lags behind the criminality of males. Second, even where females have increased their criminal activity, such changes have been relatively small and offer no immediate threat to the male domination over crime. Third, there is no simple or direct link between female criminality and such factors as modernization or female labor force participation. If these factors are important, their influence is probably indirect. And finally, comparative studies are currently handicapped by more than limited sources of data. The meaning and interpretation of such things as "emancipation" not only differs from one researcher to the next but may have different implications for female criminality from one culture to the next. Such conceptual issues are, of course, also present in studies which limit themselves to one country, but they are brought into sharp relief in cross-national research. The data used in these studies are so suspect that it is tempting to criticize them on methodological grounds and dismiss their findings. The reality, however, is that even with its inadequacies, INTERPOL data remain the only source of international crime data collected over a number of years in a relatively standardized format. Thus, the fundamental question is whether inadequate data are better than no data at all for making international comparisons.

## Case Studies of Female Criminality

While no single source of data exists as a substitute for the material collected by INTERPOL, it is possible to make general international comparisons by using a number of individual case studies. The following discussion focuses upon those individual countries for which the most information is currently available.

### England and Wales

At about the same time that Rita Simon and Freda Adler were providing the foundation for American debates about female criminality, Carol Smart was providing the groundwork for British research. Unlike either Simon or Adler, Smart (1976; 1977) focused on the ideology underlying explanations for female criminality, arguing that most were sexist images of female offenders as creatures who are biologically driven to crime. She also utilized official crime data to determine trends in female criminality from the 1930s through the 1970s, a longer time span than was possible with data from the United States. Smart (1979) concluded that increases in female criminality beginning in the 1960s were simply part of long-term fluctuations in the crime rate, which could be traced back to World War II. Given this long-term trend, she argued that contemporary increases were not likely to have resulted from the women's movement. The value of Smart's work was her methodical critique of existing thinking about female criminality, reminding us again that explanations of crime often reflect the political climate in which they are formulated.

Austin (1981) has re-analyzed the data used by Smart and concluded that, in fact, there was support for the idea that female criminality was tied to the movement for women's liberation which arose in the 1960s. He noted that for serious offenses, including violence against the person, sexual offenses, burglary and robbery, "it is precisely the 1965-75 decade which shows the greatest percentage increase for females relative to males (1981:371)." Interestingly, Austin recognized that the data could be interpreted in one of several ways but chose to argue for the influence of women's liberation on *ideological* grounds. He conceded that advocating an association between liberation and crime may support anti-liberation sentiments, but believed that the threat posed by biological arguments was even more ominous:

However, clear evidence of a relationship between the movement and female criminality blunts the biological argument because it suggests that social arrangements which the movement is changing explain much of the behavioral difference between the sexes (1981:373).

Arguing that the inconsistent findings regarding the link between liberation and crime were primarily the result of methodological flaws in the research, Box and Hale (1983) undertook a more complex analysis of factors associated with changes in both male and female criminality. They concluded that social circumstances common to both men and women were more important in accounting for crime than was a sex-specific factor, such as female liberation. They noted that the growing numbers of females on the police force was a better predictor of changes in female criminality than other indicators of changing female roles, suggesting that "much of the apparent increase in female violent crimes is probably a reflection of changing attitudes towards such [i.e. female] offenders and how they should be dealt with properly by the criminal justice system (1983:43)."

Farrington and Morris (1983) examined British arrest and court data to test the idea that women were receiving more lenient treatment than men for similar offenses. In addition to the type of crime involved, they considered such factors as prior convictions and home environment. They found that women were given lighter sentences and were less likely to be convicted again in the two years following their first offense. "However, these sex differences disappeared after allowing for the fact that women committed less serious offenses and were less likely to have been previously convicted (1983:2477)."

Finally, Carlen (1982; 1983; 1985) conducted intensive interviews with women in British prisons. Like Smart and Austin, Carlen was very sensitive to the ideological issues involved in explaining the involvement of females in the criminal justice system. She argued that many of the women in prison did not belong there because of the minor nature of their offenses, and that each phase of the justice system responds to stereotypical images of "bad" and "good" women. She believed that women who violated traditional sex-roles were particularly likely to be seen as "bad," and to consequently receive harsher punishments.

Where data and official crime statistics are presented, the image of female criminality in Great Britain is strikingly similar to that in the United States. What distinguishes British studies is their greater emphasis on the political implications of utilizing particular explanations for female criminality.

## Australia and New Zealand

What literature exists on female criminality in Australia and New Zealand closely follows that in the U.S. and Great Britain in both form and substance. Compared with the U.S. and Great Britain, however, crime data are less readily available in Australia, and research on female criminality is only beginning (Hiller, 1982). The lack of theoretical and empirical work is slowly being remedied, however. Mukherjee and Scutt (1981), for example, provide a collection of articles on various aspects of women in the criminal justice system in Australia, ranging from discussions of sexism in criminal law to the treatment of women in the Australian prison system. By and large, the conclusions of existing research mirror those of studies in the U.S. and Great Britain. There is no evidence in the Australian research for a "new breed" of violent female offender, or of increases in female property crime beyond those also noted for males (Hiller, 1982; Mukherjee and Fitzgerald, 1981).

## The Netherlands

Several studies have examined female criminality in the Netherlands. Marshall (1983) studied Dutch arrest data for the period 1958-1977 and found that female involvement in crimes of personal violence declined over the twenty year period while the male rate was relatively stable. In fact, the relative gap between males and females increased during this time for stereotypically masculine crimes, and while the gender gap narrowed for embezzlement, this was due to a faster decline in male arrests. Similarly, Bruinsma, Dessaur and Van Hezewijk (1981) found that the conviction rate declined from 1947 to 1973 for both sexes and that the decline was even greater for females than for males. They also discussed self-report studies which suggested that both males and females who commit offenses have about the same likelihood of being detected and arrested (about 3 in 1000). Shoplifting accounts for half of all offenses committed by women in the Netherlands and females who commit such property offenses are more likely than males to continue this behavior for much of their life. Consistent with Simon's (1975) opportunity theory, employment was associated with criminality, at least for women beyond their teenage years:

> Employed women average the largest number of offenses and are least confined to one type of offense. Housewives are the least "criminal," and if they commit an offense, they largely

confine themselves to a single type of offense (Bruinsma, Dessaur and Van Hezewijk, 1981:39).

In addition, the higher the level of employment the more likely a woman was to have committed an offense.

Both studies suggest that female criminality is declining in the Netherlands and that for those offenses where changes are occurring, the gap between the sexes is actually growing. Female crime in the Netherlands, as in most countries of the world, consists predominantly of minor property offenses and provides little support for the idea that contemporary female offenders have somehow become "masculinized."

## *Other Countries*

Aside from the countries already discussed, there are few nations about which an extensive body of literature on female criminality has been established. The first collection of studies from countries throughout the world was published in 1981 by Freda Adler and contains reports from 14 countries, representing six continents. In closing our discussion of case studies, we will briefly draw on some of the more interesting illustrations presented in Adler's collection, focusing particular attention on countries which have experienced rapidly changing female roles or which have restructured their legal system to guarantee equal opportunities for females.

Finland is a particularly interesting country for our purposes since it has a relatively long history of providing legal equality for the sexes. In fact, Finland was the first country in Europe to support women's suffrage, which was granted in 1906 (Anttila, 1981). Despite the early recognition of women as legally equal to men, female criminality is infrequent relative to that of men. Further, there is little evidence that female criminality in Finland is changing; when increases have been noted, they tend to be accompanied by even larger increases in male criminality. Further, women have comprised a relatively constant proportion of the prison population, ranging from two to three percent of the total. Anttila (1981) points out, that despite legal equality of the sexes, women's domestic roles have changed little since the turn of the century. Most women are still responsible for housekeeping and for raising children. This suggests that social equality is probably more important than legal equality in shaping the character of female crime, and that changes in the legal status of women are not always successful in bringing about changes in custom.

In Poland, the emancipation of women began soon after World War II. Like the emancipation of women in Finland, "It was an economic, socio-occupational emancipation; cultural and psychological changes have not really followed accordingly (Plenska, 1981:135)." Unlike many other countries, women in Poland do have full employment opportunities; most women work outside the home and having children does not stop women from working outside the home. While female criminality did rise during the 1950s (in the decade of massive societal changes regarding women), female criminality decreased steadily in the 1960s and 1970s to their previous levels. As is true in most countries, female criminality in Poland remains nonviolent and infrequent when compared with the criminality of males.

Finally, Japan represents a nonwestern culture which experienced rapid changes in the role of women following World War II. In 1946 Japan enacted a new constitution which guarantees equality of men and women under the law. The new constitution led to massive restructuring of many civil and criminal laws, including those related to marriage, guardianship, education, and election to public offices (Sato, 1981:261). These massive changes seemed to have had little influence on female criminality, however. While females have constituted a growing share of the offender population, this change has been primarily due to *decreases* in male criminality. What increases were observed for females related primarily to theft.

> We may conclude, then, that far-reaching postwar changes in women's social positions in the Japanese society seem to have had little influence upon the criminality of women in both qualitative and quantitative perspectives (Sato, 1981:263).

Thus, even in societies in which the legal status of women has changed far more dramatically than in the U.S., there has been little change in female criminality. It is important to recognize, however, that sweeping legal changes which mandate egalitarian treatment of the sexes do not inevitably lead to a cultural redefinition of women's proper roles. Even large increases in labor force participation by women do not necessarily correspond to an abandonment or redefinition of their domestic roles.

## Summary

> One proposition that is generally accepted in the study of crime and criminals is that the total number of female criminals is less than the total number of male criminals. This proposition seems to hold, whatever the ideology of the particular society, whether it is capitalist, socialist, communist, or fascist (Oloruntimehin, 1981:160).

As our discussion has shown, the world picture of female criminality which has emerged is similar whether one uses international crime data, such as that provided by INTERPOL, or focuses on case studies of individual countries. Not only is female criminality less frequent than that of males, but there is little evidence of dramatic changes in the nature or extent of crimes by women. Where the frequency of female crime has changed, similar patterns of change are generally noted for males.

These international studies have important implications for our explanations of female crime. Austin (1981) correctly noted that identifying important social factors which relate to female criminality would largely blunt biological arguments. In fact, however, we have seen that across a variety of cultural and temporal settings females are less criminal than males. Observing similarly stable patterns between age and crime has led Hirschi and Gottfredson (1983) to conclude that biological explanations for the age-crime association cannot be ruled out. Our current discussion suggests a similar conclusion regarding the association between sex and crime.

Further, to the extent that social factors do shape the nature and extent of crime, these factors do not appear sex-specific. Within any given country, a rise or fall in female criminality is generally accompanied by a corresponding rise or fall in male criminality. Even when the *extent* of change is greater for one sex, the *direction* of change is nearly always similar for the sexes. This suggests that the same factors bring about changes in both male and female criminality, and that a theory which successfully explains male crime will also explain female crime.

Finally, the nature of the data precludes firm or absolute statements about female criminality throughout the world. Many countries do not collect or report crime data and definitions of crime vary from one country to the next. Further, in only a handful of countries have researchers moved beyond the use of aggregate national data. Thus, we have little understanding of the social context in which crimes are committed by females and in which women are processed through the criminal justice system. This situation is not likely to improve in the foreseeable future and the hope that our understanding of female criminality will be dramatically improved by studying crime in other countries will probably be unmet for some time to come.

# References

Adler, F. (1977). The interaction between women's emancipation and female criminality: A cross-cultural perspective. *International Journal of Criminology and Penology, 5*, 101-112.

Adler, F. (Ed.) (1981). *The incidence of female criminality in the contemporary world*. New York: New York University Press.

Anttila, I. (1981). Female criminality in Finland—What do the statistics show? In F. Adler (Ed.), *The incidence of female criminality in the contemporary world*. New York: New York University Press.

Austin, R. (1981). Liberation and female criminality in England and Wales. *British Journal of Criminology, 21*(4), 371-374.

Bhanot, M.L., & Misra, S. (1981). Criminality amongst women in India: A study of female offenders and female convicts. In F. Adler (Ed.), *The incidence of female criminality in the contemporary world*. New York: New York University Press.

Bowker, L.H. (1978). *Women, crime, and the criminal justice system*. Lexington, MA: Lexington Books.

Box, S. & Hale, C. (1983). Liberation and female criminality in England and Wales. *British Journal of Criminology, 23*(1), 35-49.

Bruinsma, G.J.N., Dessaur, C.I., & Van Hezewijk, R.W.J.V. (1981). Female criminality in the Netherlands. In F. Adler (Ed.), *The incidence of female criminality in the contemporary world*. New York: New York University Press.

Carlen, P. (1982). Papa's discipline: An analysis of disciplinary modes in the Scottish Women's Prison. *Sociological Review, 30*(1), 97-124.

Carlen, P. (1983). *Women's imprisonment: A study in social control*. London: Routledge & Kegan Paul.

Carlen, P. (1985). *Criminal women*. Cambridge: Polity Press.

Chang, E. (1982, June 26). Chinese often kill baby girls. *The Oregonian*, p. 4, 5.

Das, M.N. (1960). Female infanticide among the Khonds of Orissa. *Man in India, 40*(1), 30-35.

Farrington, D.P. & Morris, A.M. (1983). Sex, sentencing, and reconviction. *British Journal of Criminology, 23*(3), 229-248.

Hartnagel, T.F. (1982). Modernization, female social roles, and female crime: A cross-national investigation. *The Sociological Quarterly, 23*(4), 477-490.

Hewlett, S.A. (1986). *A lesser life: The myth of women's liberation in America*. New York: William Morrow and Company.

Hiller, A.E. (1982). Women, crime and criminal justice: The state of current theory and research in Australia and New Zealand. *Australian and New Zealand Journal of Criminology, 15*(2), 69-89.

Hindelang, M.J. (1979). Sex differences in criminal activity. *Social Problems, 27*(2), 143-156.

Hirschi, T. & Gottfredson, M. (1983). Age and the explanation of crime. *American Journal of Sociology, 89*(3):552-584.

International Criminal Police Organization (INTERPOL) (1950-1982). *International Crime Statistics*. St. Cloud, France: INTERPOL.

Lee, G.R. (1984). The utility of cross-cultural data. *Journal of Family Issues, 5*(4), 519-541.

Malcolm, A.H. (1977, September 30). Japanese Red Army's hijacking and its demands said to reflect political and financial desperation. *New York Times*, p. 3.

Mansour surfaces to deny bombing jet (1986, April 6). *The Chicago Tribune*, p. 9.

Marshall, I.H. (1982). Women, work, and crime: An international test of the emancipation hypothesis. *International Journal of Comparative and Applied Criminal Justice, 6*(1), 25-37.

Marshall, I.H. (1983). The women's movement and female criminality in the Netherlands. In I.L. Barak-Glanz and E.H. Johnson (Eds.), *Comparative criminology*. Beverly Hills: Sage.

Mukherjee, S.K. & Fitzgerald, R.W. (1981). The myth of rising female crime. In S. K. Mukherjee and J.A. Scutt (Eds.), *Women and crime*. Sydney, Australia: Australian Institute of Criminology.

Mukherjee, S.K. & Scutt, J.A. (1981). *Women and crime*. Sydney, Australia: Australian Institute of Criminology.

Nash, J.R. (1981). *Look for the woman*. New York: M. Evans and Co.

Oloruntimehin, O. (1981). A preliminary study of female criminality in Nigeria. In F. Adler (Ed.), *The incidence of female criminality in the contemporary world*. New York: New York University Press.

Plenska, D. (1981). The criminality of women in Poland. In F. Adler (Ed.), *The incidence of female criminality in the contemporary world*. New York: New York University Press.

Sato, K.S. (1981). Emancipation of woman and crime in Japan. In F. Adler (Ed.), *The incidence of female criminality in the contemporary world*. New York: New York University Press.

Simon, R.J. (1975). *The contemporary woman and crime*. Washington, D.C.: U.S. Government Printing Office.

Simon, R.J. & Sharma, N. (1979). Women and crime: Does the American experience generalize? In F. Adler and R. J. Simon (Eds.), *The criminology of deviant women*. Boston: Houghton-Mifflin.

Smart, C. (1976). *Women, crime and criminology: A feminist critique*. London: Routledge & Kegan Paul.

Smart, C. (1977). Criminological theory: its ideology and implications concerning women. *British Journal of Sociology, 28*(1), 89-100.

Smart, C. (1979). The new female criminality: Reality or myth? *British Journal of Criminology, 19*(1), 50-59.

Wilson, N.K. (1983).    An international perspective on women and criminology. In E. H. Johnson (Ed.), *International handbook of contemporary developments in criminology: General issues and the Americas.* Westport, CN: Greenwood Press.

# 3

# Gender and Justice

## Introduction

Bridget Bishop, the first witch hanged in Salem, in 1692, was a non-traditional woman. She would not be dominated by any one of her three husbands. She operated an unlicensed tavern where visitors congregated late at night to play the illegal game of shuffleboard, and she dressed provocatively—some of her contemporaries might say whorishly—in a red paragon bodice. Once she had driven an accusatory stranger off her porch with a spade. Like so many other alleged witches, Bishop protested her innocence, asserting, "I know not what a witch is." (Koehler, 1980, 400).

In the case of Bridget Bishop, and other women convicted of witchcraft, the early American criminal courts displayed the extreme of gender bias. In 1986, according to the New York Task Force on Women in the Courts: "gender bias against women litigants, attorneys, and court employees is still a pervasive problem with grave consequences. Women are often denied equal justice, equal treatment and equal opportunity." Sex-based bias has been documented at every stage in the judicial process (Wikler, 1980), but that does not mean that U.S. courts are consistently and uniformly biased against women. Sometimes men are treated more harshly in court; in other cases women receive discriminatory treatment (Ghali & Chesny-Lind, 1986).

Since 1970 there have been radical changes in the laws affecting the separate spheres of men and women (Atkins & Hoggett, 1984). But, when women have challenged their discriminatory treatment in court, the results have been inconsistent as well as inconclusive. Even when women win suits for differential treatment in one court, the decision is seldom binding in other courts. Sometimes court decisions in favor of women have been so narrowly interpreted that they have not led to any significant gains in enforcement of equal treatment for women. Other court wins for women have been undone by contradictory legislation which promotes sex as a special category (Temin, 1973).

Many people think that women have an advantage in court because of the patronizing attitude of the judiciary toward females. What appears to some to be "chivalry" for women treated leniently in court may be viewed as a means for enforcing the subordinate economic position of women in our country (Moulds, 1980). In some court cases, the subordinate position of women has been justified since women are seen as naturally less responsible than men (Atkins & Hoggett, 1984). Historically, women have also constituted a reasonable class for discrimination because of, "...matters touching on the perpetration and virility of the species," a class based discrimination holding women *more* responsible than men for the care of children (Temin, 1973).

## Paternalism

The American legal system has historically treated women as inferiors (Moulds: 1980, 1982). The judiciary represents a paternal authority, and chivalry is the means of enforcing subjugation to that authority. Although courts may appear to be lenient and protective toward women, in fact, chivalry applies only for those women who are perceived as acting in accordance with sex role stereotypes for behavior (Bernstein, Cardascia & Ross, 1979). The case of Lizzie Borden makes a notorious example. Although the evidence pointed to her guilt, she was acquitted because she was "a lady". Her appearance in court with highly esteemed lawyers, wearing lace gloves and an air of fragility, made it unlikely that the jury would convict her of patricide (Jones, 1980).

When women are given lenient treatment in court because of mitigating circumstances, oftentimes those circumstances have to do with traditional roles as mother and wife. In effect, leniency supports structural inequalities between the sexes and exploitation of women (Eaton, 1983).

Women are actually treated more leniently than men because their familial labor is ideologically and materially more indispensable than men's (Daly, 1983). Punitive treatment for women would be viewed as disruptive to the nuclear family (Steffensmeier & Kramer, 1982).

## Constitutional Issues

There are two significant constitutional issues at stake in judicial bias against women. The first issue has to do with the right to privacy which is implied in the constitution and has been spelled out in numerous supreme court decisions. The other issue concerns fourteenth amendment rights to due process and equal treatment (Goldstein, 1979).

## Right to Privacy

Two controversies have arisen from the issue of privacy: abortion and birth control. Both have to do with procreation. The debate concerns females' autonomy over their bodies. The conflict over abortion has not been settled in the courts, or in the clinics, even though the Supreme Court held that laws prohibiting abortion are unconstitutional in 1973 (Roe v. Wade): "No state may impose criminal penalties on the obtaining of a safe abortion in the first trimester of pregnancy (Goldstein, 1979:361)." In other words, women cannot be given a criminal charge for obtaining an abortion, but administrative regulations and legal penalties may still prevent it.

The second controversy has to do with access to birth control and birth control information. By 1987, there may be wide-spread agreement that a woman has the right to prevent pregnancy while participating in sexual intercourse. But historically, control over procreation has been considered the perogative of the male. Many females have been denied access to birth control without the permission of their husbands or fathers. Even now, there is still controversy over whether women offenders and mental patients have the right to choose or reject birth control methods. Also, teenagers may still be discouraged from using birth control methods because they cannot get them without permission from their parents.

## Equal Protection

Until the 1970s the Supreme Court was committed to treating sex as a category which called for special treatment. Certain sex based characteristics were seen as naturally calling for different handling and separate standards. Probably the most obvious of all sex based characteristics is pregnancy. Different treatment for women was usually rationalized with reference to women's roles as bearers of children and nurturers for the family. But women's important role has not always meant benefit. Pregnancy also provides the legal rationale for economic discrimination and exclusion for women, despite the Supreme Court's finding (Cleveland v. LaFleur): "No state may fire someone from a job for which she is competent, just because she is pregnant (Goldstein, 1979:361)."

Another sex based characteristic is age of majority, since females mature more rapidly than males in our culture. But some laws made the age of adult status older for females than males. Such laws were based on the chivalrous concept of protection for the "weaker sex." But, rather than enhancing the life quality for females, protective legislation led to status inferiority and diminished autonomy.

Some discrimination against females has been based on other less obvious differences between the sexes.   Gender-based exclusion was legitimated in some schools and certain occupations before the 1970s despite law suits by females.   Supreme court decisions during the period from 1971 through 1975 are considered very significant in changing the potential career status of females in the U.S.

The question of equal pay for women for equal labor has been hotly debated in and out of court.   This issue has several components.   The economic component is very significant for women because without equal pay guarantees, their work can be devalued and access to economic power can be systematically denied them legally.   There is a reproductive component to the issue of equal pay since women are sometimes denied access to opportunities because of pregnancy or child care needs.   Still another component of the equal pay issue has to do with the social roles of women.  Without the protection of equal pay for equal work women can be relegated to an inferior status in the labor market because of their sex.

Although women were given the right to vote by the 19th amendment in 1920, even as late as 1970 there were states where all-male juries were the rule (Eastwood, 1975).   Many states had policies which included women "volunteers only," but there were no such policies for men.   The policies called for women to sign a statement that despite their responsibilities at home, they wished to serve as a member of a jury.

Both of the constitutional issues, privacy and equal treatment, were used to justify protection for females as a special status (Goldstein, 1979). However, maintaining that status depended on acting in the proper role of wife and mother.  The philosophy of the court has sometimes legitimated a "benign" bias against women, supported the traditional exclusion of women from economic power, lent authority to the subjugation of women in the patriarchal family, and authorized taking away the autonomy of women over their own procreative function.

## Leniency for Women

The sex bias in the criminal courts affects and is affected by the status of women in society.  Researchers have examined all the stages of criminal processing to determine the nature and extent of sex bias in criminal proceedings, but there has been little agreement among them (Nagel & Hagan, 1983; Lambert, 1982; Farrington & Morris, 1983).   Some have found bias favoring women at specific stages in the criminal justice process, while others have found none or even bias favoring men (Frazier, Bock & Henretta, 1983; Farrington & Morris, 1983; Kruttschnitt, 1985). It is not clear that women receive consistent treatment one way or the other at most stages in the criminal process.

However, there is one stage in the criminal proceedings in which lenient treatment for women has been consistently documented: the sentencing phase (Nagel, 1981; Parisi, 1982; Curran, 1983; Wilbanks, 1986). Women receive significantly shorter sentences than men, and they are significantly less likely to spend any time behind bars. Whether that bias comes from judges' traditional opinions about the feminine role of wife and mother (Crites, 1978) or whether the bias has to do with less serious crimes and fewer prior charges for women offenders (Farrington & Morris, 1983) is a question that remains unanswered.

Lenient treatment for females accused of crime varies with different types of crime and women criminals. Some of the factors that interact with sex in producing bias in the judicial process are: type of crime, race of those involved and the age of the accused.

## Type of Crime

Women cannot expect lenient treatment in court if they are accused of a crime which is considered "manly" such as robbery or assault (Parisi, 1982). Apparently women whose crimes violate gender roles or appear less traditional are likely to receive harsher outcomes when convicted (Zingraff & Thomson, 1984; Nagel, 1981). When women are accused of murder, though, it is not clear what they can expect. Chamblin (1979) found sex bias in favor of females in the death penalty, but Wilbanks (1983) found no evidence of disparity in the treatment of the female homicide offender.

Prostitution is a type of crime in which the bias of the criminal process obviously works to the disadvantage of females. Women continue to be singled out for prosecution in a crime that involves many more men than women (Bernat, 1985). There are two areas of differential treatment of female prostitutes: gender-based statutes which discriminate against women, and differential enforcement of the law which leads to only females being arrested (Moulds, 1982). An example of statutes with gender-based bias are those which prohibit "soliciting." On the surface, such policies which prohibit prostitutes from approaching potential customers on the street are meant to keep prostitution from becoming a public nuisance. Yet in practice, these policies make it legal for men to approach females to buy sexual services, but illegal for women to approach anyone for the purpose of selling (Sumner, 1981).  Laws against soliciting discriminate against lower status prostitutes (street walkers).

Witchcraft provides one further example of a crime which was traditionally defined in gender-biased statutes and enforced by practices which discriminated against women.  Nelson (1975) points out that a witch is the stereotype of the "bad woman" who has taken the devil for a lover. The example of Bridget Bishop, in the Introduction above, points out that women who violate gender roles can expect anything but lenient treatment when they are accused of crime.

## Race

Although sex is a very important variable affecting the outcome in court processing, race may have just as much significance as sex (Frederick & Zimmerman, 1983; Foley & Rasche, 1979).  Black females are more likely than white females to be involved in crime (Lewis, 1981).   Also, the sentences of black women are more comparable to the sentences of white men than white women (Spohn, et al, 1985).  Black males suffer the most criminal victimization and the harshest judicial treatment of all (Collier & Smith, 1981).

## Age

Another factor which has a significant impact on the outcome of criminal proceedings is the age of the offender.  But the effect of age is intricately interwoven with the effect of sex resulting in a bias against older men and younger women.

Shichor (1985) found that elderly females may be treated more leniently when accused of a crime, but elderly males do not seem to be given the same advantage.  On the other end of the spectrum, juvenile females are 170 percent more likely than male juvenile offenders to be referred to the court for status offenses, such as running away and disobeying parents.  And female status offenders receive more restrictive dispositions than males (Smith, 1980).   According to Hancock and Chesny-Lind, the double standard of juvenile justice is an international phenomenon.  Girls are subjected to more supervision than boys for less serious offenses throughout the world (Webb, 1984).

# Summary

The history of the judicial treatment of women parallels the history of the status of women in American economic and social life.  Apparent leniency for wives and mothers has been offset by strictly harsh treatment of women who deviate from stereotypical sex role expectations.  That harsh treatment is likely to begin with juvenile females accused of status offenses. It carries over to non-white women and women outside the traditional roles of the white middle class. Being female may have an impact on the outcome of an offender's criminal proceedings, but her race and economic status may have a greater one.

We can expect that the future of the criminal court will continue to parallel trends in social and economic life.  In that regard, both Kempinen (1983) and Steffensmeier (1980) have found that sex differences in the handling of criminal defendants are diminishing and they both predict that disparity in the treatment of males and females will continue to diminish in years to come.

In the future, according to Crites (1978), equal treatment for both sexes in court could result in longer periods of incarceration for females before and after sentencing, but, at present, women are likely to be convicted of less serious crimes than men and less likely to have a record of prior crimes.  So, unless the nature of women's crime changes significantly in the future, differences in sentence length may very well persist even when discretion in the sentencing decision is limited.

Leniency for women who are mothers is discriminatory against women who are not, as well as discriminatory against fathers.  But concern for the dependent children of convicted offenders must continue to be considered in criminal courts when sentencing is planned.  As time goes on, fathers may come to take more of the responsibility for nurturing children and become more indispensable to family life.  If so, then we may hope that the well-being of the family will be a greater concern in court than the sex of the offender.

# REFERENCES

Atkins, S. & Hoggett, B. (1984). *Women and the law.* New York: Basil Blackwell.

Bernat, F. (1985). New York state's prostitution statute — Case study of the discriminatory application of a gender neutral law. In C. SchWeber and C. Feinman (Eds.), *Criminal Justice, Politics and Women.* New York: Haworth Press.

Bernstein, I., Cardascia, J. & Ross, C. (1979). Defendant's sex and criminal court decisions. In R. Alvarez and K. Lutterman (Eds.), *Discrimination in organizations.* San Francisco: Jossey-Bass, Inc.

Boneparth, E. (Ed.), (1982). *Women, power and policy,* Elmsford, NY: Pergamon Press.

Butler, A. (1982). *Dispositions, pleas and sentencing in metro.* Ann Arbor: University of Michigan Institute for Social Research.

Chamblin, M. (1979). Effect of sex on the imposition of the death penalty. New York: Paper Presented At *Extra-legal Attributes Affecting Death Penalty Sentencing Symposium.* (Available from National Criminal Justice Reference Service, Rockville, MD. ACCN# 061529)

Collier, B. & Smith, W. (1981). Crime victims and offenders — A question of race and sex. *Urban League Review,* 6(1), 46-54.

Crites, L. (1978). Women in the criminal court. In W. Hepperle & L. Crites (Eds.), *Women in the courts.* Williamsburg, VA: National Center for State Courts.

Curran, D. (1983). Judicial discretion and defendant's sex. *Criminology,* 21(1), 41-58.

Daly, K. (1983). *Order in the court — Gender and justice.* Washington, DC: National Institute of Justice.

Eastwood, M. (1975). Feminism and the law. In J. Freeman, (Ed.), *Women: A feminist perspective.* Palo Alto, CA: Mayfield Publishing Co.

Eaton, M. (1983). Mitigating circumstances—Familiar rhetoric. *International Journal of the Sociology of Law*, 11(4), 385-400.

Farrington, D. & Morris, A. (1983). Sex, sentencing and reconviction. *British Journal of Criminology*, 23(3). 229-248.

Fenster, C. & Mahoney, A. (1981). Effect of prior record upon the sentencing of male-female co-defendants. *Justice System Journal*, 6(2), 262-271.

Foley, L. & Rasche, C. (1979). Effect of race on sentence, actual time served and final disposition of female offenders. In J. Conley (Ed.) *Theory and research in criminal justice—Current perspectives*. Cincinnati, OH: Anderson Publishing Co.

Frazier, C., Bock, E. & Henretta,J. (1983). Role of probation officers in determining gender differences in sentencing severity. *Sociological Quarterly*, 24(2), 305-318.

Frederick, B. & Zimmerman, S. (1983). *Discrimination and the decision to incarcerate*. Albany: New York State Division of Criminal Justice Services Office of Program Development and Research.

Ghali, M., & Chesny-Lind, M. (1986). Gender bias and the criminal justice system. *Sociology and Social Research*, 70(2), 164-171.

Goldstein, L. F. (1979). *The constitutional rights of women*. New York: Longman.

Hancock, L. & Chesny-Lind, M. (1982). Female status offenders and justice reforms—An international perspective. *Australian and New Zealand Journal of Criminology*, 15(2), 109-122.

Jones, Ann (1980). *Women who kill*. New York: Holt, Rinehart & Winston.

Jolly, M. (1979). Young, female, and outside the law—A call for justice for the girl 'delinquent.' In R. Crow & G. McCarthy (Eds.), *Teenage women in the juvenile justice system—changing values*. Tucson, AZ: New Directions For Young Women, Inc.

Kempinen, C. (1983), Changes in the sentencing patterns of male and female criminal defendants. *The Prison Journal*, 632, 3-11.

Koehler, L. (1980). *A search for power.* Urbana: University of Illinois Press.

Kruttschnitt, C. (1985). Legal outcomes and legal agents. *Law and Human Behavior,* 9(3), 287-303.

Lewis, D. (1981). Black women offenders and criminal justice. In M. Warren (Ed.), *Comparing female and male offenders.* Beverly Hills: Sage.

Lambert, S. (1982). *Court process in rivertown.* Ann Arbor: University of Michigan Institute for Social Research.

Moulds, E. (1980). Chivalr· ·nd paternalism: Disparities of treatment in the criminal justice system. In S. Datesman & F. Scarpitti (Eds.), *Women, crime and justice.* New York: Oxford University Press.

Moulds, E. (1982). Women's crime, women's justice. In E. Boneparth (Ed.), *Women power and policy.* Elmsford, NY: Pergamon Press.

Nagel, I. (1981). Sex differences in the processing of criminal defendants. In A. Morris & L. Gelsthorpe (Eds.), *Women and crime.* Cambridge, U.K.: University of Cambridge Institute of Criminology.

Nagel, I. & Hagan, J. (1983). Gender and crime: Offense patterns and criminal court sanctions. In M. Tonry and N. Morris (Eds.), *Crime and Justice: An Annual Review, Vol. 4* Chicago: University of Chicago Press.

Nelson, M. (1975). Why witches were women. In J. Freeman, (Ed.), *Women – A feminist perspective.* Palo Alto, CA: Mayfield Publishing Co.

New York Task Force on Women in the Courts, (1986). New York: Office of Court Administration.

Parisi, N. (1982). Are females treated differently? In N. Rafter & E. Stanko (Eds.), *Judge, lawyer, victim, thief.* Boston: NorthEastern University Press.

Pisciotta, A. (1983). Race, sex and rehabilitation: A study of differential treatment in the juvenile reformatory, 1825- 1900. *Crime and Delinquency,* 29(2), 254-269.

Popiel, M. (1980). Sentencing women – Equal protection in the context of discretionary decision making. *Women's Rights Law Reporter,* 6(1-2), 85-106.

Shichor, D. (1985).   Male/female differences in elderly arrests. *Justice Quarterly*, 2(3), 399-414.

Smith, D. (1980).   *Young female offenders—Analysis of differential handling based on sex—Special report* Pittsburgh: National Center for Juvenile Justice.

Spohn, C, et. al., (1985).   Women defendants in court: the interaction between sex and race in convicting and sentencing. *Social Science Quarterly*, 66(1), 178-185.

Steffensmeier, D. (1980).   Assessing the impact of the women's movement on sex-based differences in the handling of adult criminal defendants. *Crime and Delinquency*, 26(3), 344-357.

Steffensmeier, D. & Kramer, J. (1982).   Sex-based differences in the sentencing of adult criminal defendants. *Sociology and Social Research*, 66(3), 289-304.

Sumner, M. (1981).   Prostitution and the position of women—A case for decriminalization. In A. Morris & L. Gelsthorpe (Eds.), *Women and crime*. Cambridge, U.K.: University of Cambridge Institute of Criminology

Temin, C. (1973).   Discriminatory sentencing of women offenders: The argument for ERA in a nutshell. *The American Criminal Law Review*, 11(2), 355-372.

Webb, D. (1984).   More on gender and justice: Girl offenders on supervision. *Sociology*, 18(3), 367-381.

Wikler, N. (1980).   On the judicial agenda for the '80s—Equal treatment for men and women in the courts. *Judicature*, 64(5), 202-209.

Wilbanks, W. (1983).   The female homicide offender in Dade County, Florida. *Criminal Justice Review*, 8(2) 9-14.

Wilbanks, W. (1986).   Are female felons treated more leniently by the criminal justice system? *Justice Quarterly*, 3(4) 517-530.

Zingraff, M. & Thomson, R. (1984).   Differential sentencing of women and men in USA. *International Journal of the Sociology of Law*, 12(4) 401-413.

# 4

# Women in Prison

## Introduction

Picture a cluster of red brick buildings perched high in a mountain meadow surrounded by lovely fields and streams. At first glance it looks like a college or a sanitarium. Take a longer look and you will discover that it is really a federal prison for women. It holds female prisoners with every classification of security level—from maximum security to community custody. It was meant to be an experimental model for women's prisons.

The history of this experiment in corrections details the history of prisons for women in the U.S. By the example of this prison for women, we can explore the historical forces which have shaped others throughout the country. A close look at this example provides an image of the structures that operate inside closed institutions for women, too. A look at the prison can also include the women held there—their lives and their crimes. These three perspectives (outside forces, inside structures, and characteristics of prisoners) are the focus for this closer look at women in prison.

## The Alderson Story

### Founding

In the federal prison system there is only one prison which is for women exclusively. It is located in an isolated river valley near Alderson, West Virginia. It first opened in 1927 when the women's prison reform movement which began around 1870 was coming to an end (Rafter, 1985; Fox, 1984). Even into the 20th century, women were often held in custodial institutions with men under abominable conditions (Rafter, 1983). Forced prostitution and rape were common.

The popular image of female offenders has had an important impact on Alderson and all prisons for women. Before 1900, incarcerated women were commonly thought of as "fallen" or "wayward," beyond hope or help (Feinman, 1983). They were sanctioned as immoral, regardless of the offenses they committed.

The image of female criminals changed gradually around the turn of the century, marked by the opening of the first reformatory for women in 1873, in Indiana, closely followed by several other states. Feminists of that time considered women criminals to be "victims of male lust." Incarcerated females were presumed to have been led astray by misguided love for a man. So, by the time Alderson was opened in 1927, a philosophy of corrections for women had been developed which had its basis in ideas of "separate but equal" (Freedman, 1981). Women could only be reformed by keeping them away from the evil influences of men. The coalition of women's groups which was responsible for opening this first federal prison for women wanted to isolate women from men, and from the harmful influences of city life, hence the remote, rural location, which is still common in both state and federal prisons for women.

In its early days, the policy at Alderson was developed by Mary Belle Harris, the first superintendant. She was supported by a large coalition of women of means and social status, so she was able to put many of her ideas about reform into practice. The founders of Alderson envisioned a "ladies' seminary," in which they would create a "society of women working together under the guidance of other women" (SchWeber, 1982: 278). Although they intended to reform women criminals by inculcating independence from men, nevertheless, the program for inmates at Alderson focused on homemaking, not economic independence. Women were involved in "men's work" such as farming, maintenance, and loading, only for institutional support. Their heavy work was thought to be therapeutic, since it consumed energy and made the inmates easier to control, not because it better prepared them to find employment after release.

When Alderson opened in 1927 it held over 200 women. The majority of those committed there were drug addicts (SchWeber, 1980). The federal prison system was affected by the Harrison Act of 1914 which made the use of narcotics illegal. At that time, many women had become addicted to opiates in the form of laudanum in "tonics." Those who continued to use opiates became criminals after laudanum was no longer available to them legally (Datesman, 1981). The early founders developed the programs at Alderson to meet the needs of women criminals who were the victims of a legal change which defined them as such and called for their incarceration. The federal narcotics laws did not have this impact on the development of state prisons for women. But, in each state, the emergence of a separate prison system for women is related to changes in legal definitions.

Three years after its opening, the "experimental nature" which had characterized Alderson also began to change. As part of a centralized, Federal Bureau of Prisons begun in 1930, Alderson's separateness was gradually, but surely, eroded. Mary Belle Harris began to feel pressure to conform to standards developed for all federal prisons, all men's prisons, that is.

## The 1950s

Alderson remained the only federal prison for women until 1955. At that time a unit for women was opened in the men's penal institution on Terminal Island, California. In the '50s, Alderson held over 600 women.

An excellent picture of Alderson in the 1950s was presented by Elizabeth Gurley Flynn (1963) a labor organizer and communist who was held there for 28 months from 1955-1957. Flynn celebrated her 65th birthday while incarcerated. She later wrote that she was moved and grateful when many of the other inmates remembered her with flowers and gifts.

After reading of the early days of Alderson, Elizabeth Gurley Flynn commented that all of Mary Belle Harris's methods and ideas had been discarded by 1955 and replaced with dull routine. For Flynn the one word that best described Alderson was "frustration." She reported that neither psychiatric treatment nor occupational therapy were offered to inmates. Women did what was ordinarily called "men's work" in the '50s, just as they had in the '30s, but it still did not prepare them for work on the outside. The 1950s was a time of racial conflict and change at Alderson. Elizabeth Gurley Flynn reflected the strife and confusion created by these changes inside prison in her account. She described instances of discrimination against staff and inmates and perpetrated by both.

Elizabeth Gurley Flynn also described the characteristics of Alderson which were unique to prisons for women. For example, the presence of pregnant women called for special treatment for those who would deliver babies while incarcerated. Flynn noted that in former years, women were allowed to keep their children with them for up to three years. By the 1950s mothers were allowed to keep their infants in prison for a few months. She added that: "the presence of a baby was a pleasant, humanizing influence."

Other characteristics unique to women's prisons were not looked on so favorably. Flynn commented: "to weep, have hysterics, shriek, scream, have 'spells', are expected behavior patterns among women in prison." She was certain that men prisoners did not behave so emotionally nor immaturely.

On the other hand, Elizabeth Gurley Flynn mentioned an aspect of prison life which was as important to men as to the women she observed. As she put it, "The most universally despised women were the stool pigeons." Clearly, she is referring to behavior that is also known as "ratting" or "snitching," and which is strongly condemned in prisons for men as well (Clemmer, 1940).

## The Present

By 1985, the population of prisoners at Alderson had grown to over 700 women, according to Federal Bureau of Prison statistics.[1] That is 25% of all the women held in federal prisons. The rest of the female federal inmates are held in co-ed facilities. At Alderson, the inmates' crimes are varied, but nearly 40% of them were convicted of drug law violations. So there are still a large proportion of women incarcerated there because of the legal status of psychoactive substances now, just as in Mary Belle Harris's time.

Alderson's status as a "Ladies Seminary" has changed, though. Now, there are as many men on the staff as women. In some ways, it has become simply another unit in the Federal Bureau of Prisons. Nearly half of the prisoners there are under 30 years of age, and 70% are non-white. Less than half of the inmates at Alderson had received a high school diploma or the equivalent (GED). Nearly half were unemployed at the time of their arrest, and approximately two thirds were charged with either property offenses or drug law violations. These characteristics are similar to those found in most prisons for males as well as females.

Being the only prison exclusively for women in the federal prison system does mean some significant differences for Alderson, compared to other federal prisons, though. For example: In 1985, there were 18 pregnant women incarcerated there. Either they were pregnant when they were convicted, or they became pregnant while on furlough, or while being held in a sexually integrated prison. There is no instance of an inmate becoming pregnant at Alderson included in the 18 pregnancies. Also, 70% of the women incarcerated at Alderson have children. Of those who have children, most have more than one child. Many of these women are single heads of households, since only 33% were married (including common-law) at the time of their arrest. Less than 10% of the prisoners listed their occupation as "housewife."

Throughout its history, Alderson has been supported by the work of women inmates. That is still true. Nearly 150 inmates work in institutional support systems such as food services and facilities operations. Housekeeping, laundry, and grounds keeping are also sources of work for a significant proportion of inmates. In the 1980s non-traditional training apprenticeships are offered to prepare women for improved employment opportunities when they are released. However, less than 50 women are involved in these programs. There are also prison industry programs offered at Alderson. They provide both training and money to participants. While they offer advantages to those who can take part in them, they are not available to everyone. In 1985, less than 200 inmates were working in prison industries. At that time, less than 50 women were learning graphics in a decal making shop. The rest of those employed by prison industries were working in a garment factory, sewing. This is the type of prison industry that is most commonly found in prisons for women in the U.S. in the 1980s.[1] In the present, as in the past, the situation at Alderson reflects the public image of female offenders in the ways women prisoners are treated there, and in the characteristics of the women held there.

Because Alderson is the one federal prison for women its history and development have been unique. Nevertheless, this prison represents many typical patterns that can be found in any women's prison in the U.S.: the women there feel their greatest personal deprivation is the loss of their children, the treatment of female prisoners in the criminal justice system reflects their status as a powerless minority, and the women incarcerated are most likely to be economic marginals without resources in society.

## Differences in Scale—Fewer Programs

Women are definitely a minority as prisoners. Only 3-4 percent of those incarcerated in state prisons in the U.S. are women. They make up about 6 percent of those in jails and federal prisons (Sargent, 1984; Ryan, 1984; Wheeler, 1974). As Table 4.1 shows, compared with males, the proportion of women prisoners has remained fairly stable since 1933.

Males stand a much greater chance of being imprisoned than women. In fact, 24 times more men are incarcerated than women in the U.S. Throughout the country men are far more likely to be incarcerated than women regardless of their race. The difference is greatest in the Northeast, where the number of white men in prison is 35 times greater than the number of white women. The difference is least between black men and women in the West, where the number of black men incarcerated is 20 times greater than the number of black women. In other words the differences range from 20-35 times greater for men than for women, whether black or white. Tables 4.1 and 4.2 spell out regional and racial differences in incarceration rates.

TABLE 4.1
Male and Female Proportions of Sentenced Prisoners
in State and Federal Institutions (1933-1983)

| Year | Total | Males | Females |
|------|-------|-------|---------|
| 1983 | 419,820 | 96% | 4% |
| 1973 | 204,211 | 97% | 3% |
| 1963 | 217,283 | 96% | 4% |
| 1953 | 173,579 | 96% | 4% |
| 1943 | 137,220 | 96% | 4% |
| 1933 | 136,810 | 97% | 4% |

Source: McGarrell & Flanagan, 1985: 647

TABLE 4.2
Regional Differences in Incarceration Rates for Males and Females

| | Ratio by Race and Sex: | | |
| Region: | male/female | white male/female | black male/female |
|---------|-------------|-------------------|-------------------|
| U.S. | 24:1 | 25:1 | 23:1 |
| Northeast | 31:1 | 35:1> | 31:1 |
| Northcentral | 21:1 | 25:1 | 21:1 |
| South | 24:1 | 25:1 | 24:1 |
| West | 22:1 | 24:1 | 20:1< |

<>greatest and smallest differences between males and females in rates per 100,000 incarcerated occur in the northeast for whites and in the west for blacks, respectively.

Source: McGarrell & Flanagan, 1985:654

Because of their relatively small numbers, women inmates have received inferior services and less meaningful programs. There is also evidence that sex-role stereotyping operates in the types of training and programs offered in many women's prisons (Bowker, 1977; CONtact, 1981). The situation at Alderson is repeated in prisons for women around the country. In some cases prison industries offer inmates opportunities for training and money for participating. Often, these opportunities are open to only a small number of prisoners. In many cases, traditional female vocational training is offered (Haft, 1980).

Although some prisons offer programs that are called "non-traditional vocational training," it is often work in support of the institution (Chandler, 1973). Historically, "men's work" has been done by women in prisons for women. It has not provided non-traditional work opportunities for the inmates' futures, so much as it has kept the institutions going.

## Inmate Subculture

Many of those who study prisons are interested in the microcosm of society that grows there. Inside a closed institution the way of life is affected by the social class, prior experiences and ties with significant others on the outside the inmates bring with them (Zingraff, 1980). Whether or not a prisoner is wealthy and has powerful contacts in society outside the prison has a strong positive impact on his or her position on the inside. A prisoner who has prior experiences with incarceration and has a history of arrests and a criminal lifestyle is also likely to have a higher status position on the inside than a prisoner who has not. Whether or not a prisoner gets letters, support, and visits from family and friends on the outside is also positively related to social position on the inside. This evidence supports an importation model for describing the subculture of prisoners. It appears, from this point of view, that factors brought with the prisoner from the outside are most important in predicting how s/he will adjust to life inside. The negative effects of adjustment to prison have been termed "prisonization" (Wheeler, 1961).

The process of "prisonization" for women has also been explained from an internal point of view. In the indigenous approach, factors within the prison itself are more important in explaining how inmates adjust to life and the subculture that develops there. The indigenous or structural approach is supported by the evidence that there are norms and folkways and traditions which develop inside prisons in a way not found elsewhere. Some of the examples which support the indigenous viewpoint are: the inmate code of rules for behavior which prohibits snitching, the leadership roles that develop from institutionally valued behavior, and the typical relationships inmates establish among themselves along with the roles they can be expected to play.

The importation model and the indigenous model depict two different sides of the inmate subculture for both men and women. Although women prisoners, like men, have developed a norm which prohibits giving information to the staff, or snitching, some researchers have found that unlike men, women prisoners are not really committed to an inmate code (Kruttschnitt, 1981, 125). Comparisons are difficult to pin down, though, since it is not really clear how committed to the inmate code men prisoners actually are either.

Leadership and status are achieved in similar ways in both men's and women's prisons—intelligence and aggression are highly valued (Moyer, 1980; Van Wormer and Bates, 1979). Researchers have found that leaders in women's prisons are likely to be incarcerated for a serious, aggressive crime. Nevertheless, the amount of actual victimization in prisons for women is much less than in prisons for men. In contrast to men's prisons, there are few rapes and much less aggressive homosexuality in the inmate subculture of women (Bowker, 1981).

One significant difference between prison subcultures for men and women is that "play families" develop in some women's prisons. In these groups, women play various family roles, but the most common "pretend" relationships are mother-daughter and sister-sister (Propper, 1982). In some prisons entire kinship structures evolve with women playing the parts of father, husband and brother as well as the female roles. The development of kinship groups in women's prisons vary with the average ages, length of sentences and isolation of the inmates. The patterns change with institutional changes (Fox, 1984, 32). At Alderson, for example, there was no mention of pseudo-families in Flynn's book in the 1950s, but they were apparently very important to the inmate subculture in the 1960s (Giallombardo, 1966).

In the present, the general characteristics of women prisoners remain very similar to those found in the '60s and '70s despite the social changes that have affected women during the past twenty years (Epperson, Hannum and Datwyler, 1982). Incarcerated women are likely to be poor, and poorly educated. They are likely to have two children and be the head of their household. Women prisoners are likely to be members of a racial or ethnic minority and charged with a property crime (CONtact, 1981).

These are the characteristics that are imported into the prison subculture. Inside the prison, the structural characteristics of the institution have an effect on the style of life that is adapted. A significant characteristic of the prison subculture is the structural element of coercion and loss of decision making power that may be seen by prisoners as an "imposition of despair" (Mahan, 1984).

Women's prisons are often more attractive in appearance than men's prisons, but the peaceful appearance may be deceptive (Moyer, 1984; Gibson, 1976). Those who are held there are constantly reminded of their status as prisoners by a multiplicity of rules and punishments. They feel the separation from their loved ones and their lives outside acutely. They may also be treated according to sexual stereotypes when recreational and vocational training is provided, if at all. It is also possible that women prisoners may be subjected to sexist medical evaluations and prescription routines. For one example, the rate of psychoactive medication is from two to ten times higher for incarcerated women than men (Shaw, 1982: 265). At Alderson, 10% of the inmates were receiving psychotropic drugs in 1984.

Both imported and indigenous characteristics play an important part in the inmate subculture. And both inside the prison and in the society outside, we can expect men and women's social roles to continue to follow different lines of development.

## Security—Rules and Punishment

Most women prisoners simply are not dangerous (Richie-Mann, 1984: 190). Since they are seldom considered a threat, the security that is involved in keeping them imprisoned is not usually justified to protect the community. Instead, because of the ideas of the early founders about "separate but equal" in women's prisons, the barriers surrounding them are necessary for another reason. That is to keep men out. Only a very small number of those women held in state and federal prisons actually need maximum security. Nevertheless, high fences and isolated, rural locations are common in institutions for women.

Since the proportion of women in each jurisdiction who are incarcerated is small, often prisoners with a variety of needs—from community custody to strictist maximum security—are held in the same prison. As a result, all the women held there are subjected to enhanced security.

The staff who work in women's prisons have an important impact on the quality of life for the inmates there. No doubt, there are many individual differences in staff-inmate relations, but research reports that female inmates are " harder to work with," in the opinions of the corrections staff (Pollack, 1984). The staff is likely to find that women inmates have more severe problems than men inmates due to the impact of incarceration on family life.

Stereotypes about women often play a part in staff-inmate relations, too. Attractiveness can be used in manipulating staff, and unattractiveness may be a disadvantage (Cavior, Hayes, Cavior, 1974: 37). It has also been reported that women receive significantly less severe punishment than men for similar disciplinary reports (Lindquist, 1980). Whatever the outcome, most of the disciplinary reports in prisons for women are not concerned with serious or dangerous behavior. Observers agree that rules and regulations are petty and minor nuisances often become major problems in prisons for women.

Women's prisons are smaller, less dangerous, more attractive and more humane than men's prisons. As a result, there are those who think of men's prisons as "real prisons" and prisons for women as something less (Hunter, 1984: 131). Ask any woman held in prison about her forced confinement, and you will hear the same answer: "It is a real prison for me."

## The Classic Studies

The 1960s were important years for the study of women's prisons (Rasche, 1975). During that decade there was an unprecedented scientific interest, and three important studies about women in prison were published from 1965 through 1972.

### Ward and Kassebaum — 1965, WOMEN'S PRISON

When David Ward and Gene Kassebaum studied a woman's prison they were unquestionably biased. In the first place, they began with the assumption that "males have more important concerns than females (76)." With that idea in mind, they concluded that since women's self-images depend on relationships with men, sexuality is their principal means for achieving success. It followed that, according to Ward and Kassebaum, "Homosexuality is the principal adaptation for women to the stress of prison life (166)." They thought of homosexuality as a "predominant compensatory response." They described the inmate subculture as a collection of homosexual pairs and friendship cliques without close ties or common goals (78).

Ward and Kassebaum saw women as "criminally immature." They found no rules prohibiting informing in a woman's prison, no inmate code. They concurred with the 19th century idea of the feminist prison reform movement: "women need different treatment from men (42)."

By their report, Ward and Kassebaum made it clear that the women they had in mind were different from the women who are likely to be found in a women's prison. According to them, "Women continue to receive financial support when a marriage is dissolved, do not compete on an equal basis with men on the job market, and continue to be principally concerned with being homemakers (71)." This is an image which is far from the reality women in prisons actually faced, then and now.

## Giallombardo — 1966, SOCIETY OF WOMEN

Rose Giallombardo had an idea about women that was remarkably similar to that held by Ward and Kassebaum. She described women as relative to men, for whom self-respect and status are due to the cultivation of a female role in service to males. Since Giallombardo believed that women were validated by attracting males, she necessarily saw relationships between women as innately competitive. She described the inmate subculture in a women's prison as, "calculated solidarity not mutual trust...the forced company of untrustworthy others (100)."

Giallombardo stated her perspective succinctly: "The concepts of endurance, loyalty and dignity are not meaningful to the female (1966B: 285)." From that point of view she studied the kinship group structures in the women inmates' subculture. In contrast to her assumption about calculated solidarity, she found that "play families" in prison link prisoners into units which serve the members' common interests. The groups consider reciprocal rights and duties and provide for economic, defense and service needs of the family. Pseudo-families are WE groups. That means that they are intimate, now-oriented, and stress doing things together.

Giallombardo also assumed that play-families were homosexual in nature. She believed that because open demonstrations of affection between women are common and easy, women are likely to have been thereby preconditioned to homosexuality.

Low levels of aggression among women prisoners led Giallombardo to assume that women do not sanction those who violate the inmate code, and also that the inmate code of silence is not significant to women. On the other hand, she described "vitriolic verbal attacks" against informers as the means of sanctioning the code, and observed that gossip is an important weapon of defense. In her conclusions about sexuality and the inmate code, Giallombardo failed to consider the multiplicity of adjustments that prisoners develop for life in a society of women.

## Heffernan – 1972, *MAKING IT IN PRISON*

Esther Heffernan also saw that preconditioning had an important impact on getting along inside prison.  She developed three categories to describe those found in a prison for women: The "square," who identify with the established order, the "cool," who identify with a more personal and opportunistic order and the "life," who identify with a criminal life style and the underworld.  The three subsystems provide female prisoners with three different sets of goals, behavioral codes and means of mutual support. Heffernan could see that women did have an inmate code.  She stated it in the maxim: *Mind Your Own Business* (89).

Heffernan could also see that women's relationships were based on a multiplicity of factors, not simply homosexuality.  She described a variety of relationships, which included close friendships and play families as well as pair bonding.  She noted that overt homosexuality was only one of many ways in which women related to women.  Heffernan's study of making it in a prison for women has proved most valid of the three because her preconceptions about women were based on the environments of the women she studied.

## Burkhart – 1973, *WOMEN IN PRISON*

One other study of women's prisons deserves mention in this series. Although her method was not scientific but rather journalistic, Katherine Burkhart developed a valid picture of the women's inmate subculture.  She used the concept of "forced dependency" to describe this subculture. Burkhart, like Heffernan, based her description on the real world of women prisoners.  She was able to see the ways in which sexual stereotypes become self-fulfilling prophesies for women in prison.

Since these studies were published there has been much more attention directed to women in prison.  In 1983-84, two entire issues of *The Prison Journal* (63/2, 64/1) were devoted to the subject.  In the 1970s and '80s many researchers became concerned with mothers in prison and their children.

## ... and their Children

### Punishing the Children

The children of inmate mothers are an important concern since the majority of women prisoners have very young, dependent children living with them at the time of their arrest (National Advisory Commission On Criminal Justice Standards & Goals, 1973: 379). In 1982, it was estimated that some quarter of a million children had mothers in prison (Bertram, 1982). Many more men are in prison, so even more fathers are incarcerated than mothers. The loss of parental support during the formulative years is significant for any child regardless of whether the lost parent is a father or a mother. Inmate mothers are more likely than inmate fathers to have been the primary caretaker for their children before their incarceration (Datesman & Cales, 1983: 142), so the loss may be critical.

The child of an inmate mother is punished along with her. The punishment is the result of neglect, usually not malicious intent, although it is certainly malicious neglect (McGowan & Blumenthal, 1978). As she passes through each stage in the Criminal Justice process, the woman charged with a crime finds policies and practices that undermine her family ties. Narrow, linear vision focused on crime and punishment omits concern for children by law enforcement officers, court officials and corrections departments. The needs of the children involved are rarely considered at all. As a result, the children of inmate mothers are likely to undergo drastic life changes, trauma and stress. In most cases, the trauma to the child is minimized when other family members are able to take custody temporarily.

Researchers have found that black prisoners may have more extended family ties to provide support for their children while they are incarcerated than whites. Both black and white inmate mothers report that they prefer their own mothers as caretakers for their children while they are in prison (Baunach, 1985). Unfortunately, maternal grandmothers are not always there to care for the children.

Most prison mothers express dissatisfaction with the way their children are being treated while they are away. Many report that their children develop behavioral and emotional problems during their mother's incarceration. Others are concerned because they know their children are being abused or neglected while they are in prison. It is impossible to say how many of the children whose mothers are in prison will someday be found in prisons themselves, but it is likely that children who are punished for the crimes of their mothers may become troubled youths and, later, troublesome adults. Narrow criminal justice policies that leave out children may be very costly in terms of the social problems which develop with each successive generation of children whose mothers are incarcerated.

## Losing Custody

Inmate mothers often have legal concerns about their children along with their concerns for their welfare. Many women are afraid they will lose custody of their children forever because of their status as a convicted felon. In some custody hearings, the fact that a mother is incarcerated is taken to mean she is abandoning the children and custody is automatically taken. As felons, in some states, women lose their civil rights and are denied some of their rights to legal challenges, although some states have revised their legal approaches to custody(Feinman, 1986). The consent of the mother is not necessarily required in adoption hearings. Mothers in prison are left out of most of the important decisions about their children's lives while they serve time, and sometimes permanently (Richie-Mann, 1984: 241).

In some cases, inmate mothers are declared unfit and custody is removed permanently for the protection of the children. Too often the standards by which unfitness is determined are vague and abuse and neglect are not documented. In other cases, the nature of the crime is used to determine the fitness of the mother, as when prostitutes are automatically considered unfit mothers.

Instead, a more considered approach to criminal justice and children has been recommended by Baunach (1984). She suggests that the fitness of female felons as mothers be determined by the relationship that was established between them and their children before their incarceration. Baunach also recommends that rather than strict definitions which link specific crimes such as prostitution with unfitness, the causal relationship between whatever crime and the ability of the mother to perform her parental role because of her involvement in the crime is the key to determining fitness. In the case of prostitution, each individual case merits investigation to determine how the prostitute related to her children as a mother, and what lifestyle they developed as a family. The happiness and best interests of the children are important considerations in determining legal custody, but they are often ignored.

## Roles as Mothers

Inmate mothers are likely to lose a major source of identity when they lose their parental role because of incarceration (Haley, 1980: 340; Kolman, 1983: 155). Some mothers may suffer from guilt and remorse at the loss of the identity, and blame themselves for the trauma their children have experienced. Others may become hostile and alienated because they blame the system for their children's experiences. In either case, the identity of an unfit mother is a difficult one to assume (Mahan, 1982).

The majority of inmate mothers would like to maintain contact with their children during their incarceration (Neto & Bainer, 1983: 125). Although visiting arrangements in women's prisons are sometimes remote and often impersonal and harsh, nevertheless most mothers would like to have visits with their children while they are serving time (Datesman & Cales, 1983: 152). Many corrections departments have developed programs which offer extended visits with children for mothers who earn the privilege by following the rules. Rather than interfering with security, visits with family members can actually enhance security and improve overall behavior.

In some prisons for women, programs have also been developed to provide special treatment for pregnant inmates. The programs are sometimes medical, educational, or vocational — or a combination of these three treatments. At the very least, pregnant inmates should be provided with adequate diets and given medical examinations regularly, but women's prisons do not always meet even this lowest standard.

Historically, prisons for women have provided for small infants to stay with their mothers while they served time together. In 1984, this was the case in New York (Ryan, 1984), but most other states have abandoned the practice except in a few exceptional cases. It is crucial to infants' well-being that they develop ties to a nurturant parent during the first few months of their lives. But in most cases, an inmate who delivers a baby while incarcerated is escorted to a hospital for a brief period, and returned shortly after giving birth. The infant is cared for by someone else and the mother may not even be allowed to touch the baby again until her release, if ever.

Two types of programs for inmate mothers, encouraging visits and keeping mothers and infants together, are feasible in prisons for women since they have been successfully implemented in the past as well as in a few cases at present. Programs that address the needs of mothers in prison are worth whatever their cost if they prevent unnecessary punishment for their children.

## Co-Ed Prisons

### Sexually Re-integrating Prisons

The movement to separate men and women prisoners ended in 1971 when the Federal Co-Correctional Institution (FCI) at Fort Worth, TX was opened as a sexually integrated prison (Campbell, 1980). Several state corrections departments also began to administer prisons to hold both men and women. In 1977, fifteen states were reported to be operating co-corrections facilities (Korba Assoc.: 15). By 1984, that number was reduced to six states where men and women were held together (Ryan: 103). Co-corrections has become a viable option for corrections administrations as more and more litigation involving equal rights for female offenders comes up in court.

Since women prisoners still comprise such a minority of the total number of offenders for which any corrections department is responsible, the extent of their integration with men is necessarily limited. SchWeber (1984) points out that many factors may serve to the disadvantage of women in co-ed prisons. There may be so many more men than women that the women may be conspicuous and face discrimination. Men are more likely to be dangerous than women, so women held in a prison for men may be threatened by violence or held in more secure confinement than is necessary. Men and women relate differently at different ages, so the ages and criminal histories of the men with whom they are locked up is important to females held with males. Disparity in release dates are also important to women in co-ed prisons. Being held with men who have consistently longer or shorter sentences affects their own adjustment.

In general, women held separately fare better than those held in special sections of prisons for males (CONtact, 1981). Haft describes women in men's prisons as being in "prisons within prisons" (1980: 325). In these arrangements great lengths are called for to keep men and women from interacting. The freedom of the women is completely restricted since they are fewest in number and easier to keep under surveillance.

By contrast, real co-ed prisons are those in which males and females are held and interact under a single administration. Naturally, the amount of interaction varies. In some prisons, men and women openly congregate and share many facilities. In others there is planned interaction in certain programs, but males and females are usually separate.

By 1985, 75% of the women incarcerated in the federal bureau of prisons were held in sexually integrated prisons. In addition to Fort Worth, TX, co-ed prisons were opened in Lexington, KY; Pleasanton, CA; and Morgantown, KY. Although women were held for some time in the Federal Prison at Terminal Island, CA after 1955, it was never considered a co-ed facility and integration of men and women was limited.

## The Co-ed Inmate Subculture

For the past 15 years, the policy of co-corrections at FCI Fort Worth has been studied extensively (Mahan, et al, 1986 & 1987). Researchers have concluded that this co-ed setting has advantages for both men and women. Violence is almost unheard of, and no aggressive homosexuality is reported. Significant relationships develop between men and women. Inmates often consider their personal relationships with the opposite sex at FCI Fort Worth to be important for rehabilitation. For women prisoners, this co-ed prison provides a greater variety of vocational training and other opportunities to prepare for economic independence than they are likely to find in prisons exclusively for women.

At FCI Fort Worth, the policy strictly limits all physical contact between inmates to holding hands. Inmates are strongly discouraged from meeting when they are released from this prison, too. These two structural limits have been important in the types of intimate relationships men and women develop as they serve time together.

Although their relationships may have structural limits, there is no limit to the depth of emotional involvement between men and women incarcerated at FCI Fort Worth. Because the relationships are necessarily short term, prisoners find they learn lessons in intimacy in brief, intense experiences. Because sexuality is prohibited, holding hands has become a significant part of intimate relationships between inmates. This intense, intimate pair bonding at FCI Fort Worth is known as a "walkie" relationship by inmates and staff. "Walkies" provide each other with companionship, support, advice, sympathy and concern. They reduce the destructiveness of prison life for both males and females in co-ed prisons.

## Co-corrections Policy

In 1984, twenty seven states were involved in litigation about equal rights for incarcerated females (Ryan: 143). Providing equally for a minority such as women in a system like corrections is a complex and ever-changing responsibility. In some cases, integrating women into men's prisons is a useful option for meeting that responsibility. However, the degree of useful integration of male and female inmates varies. Rather than co-ed prisons, sometimes co-ordinate prisons are called for (Campbell, 1982). In this case, women retain some of their separateness, but are able to share facilities with men.

There are certain issues that must be considered, though, if sexually integrated prisons are ever really to meet the needs of incarcerated females:

> The ideal ratio of female to male prisoners in a sexually integrated prison is 50-50. When the difference in the ratio of females to males is greater than 40-60 or 60-40 the co-ed policy loses its effectiveness.

> Those held together must be classified as similar. Drastic differences in ages and backgrounds between males and females interferes with the effectiveness of sexual integration.

The administration of a co-ed prison must include females as well as males in decision making positions. Women are usually at a disadvantage in a prison run strictly by men regardless of the policy.

A co-ed prison must provide opportunities for real interaction between males and females with equal status. For primary, helping relationships to develop between men and women they must associate in the settings of everyday life: meals, work, learning, play, etc. However, overt and offensive sexuality must be discouraged, sanctions for homosexuality must be equal to those for heterosexuality, inmate-staff sexual involvement must be discouraged and pregnancies during incarceration must be avoided.

The four issues of proportionality, similarity, power, and sexuality are important to the interests of female offenders serving time in sexually integrated prisons. These issues must be considered if this policy is to be useful for women, or for men.

## Community Corrections

After their release from prison, female inmates continue to comprise only a small proportion of offenders on parole. In 1978 less than 6% of those on parole in the U.S. were women (NCCD, 1980). Convicted women in the community have seldom been the subject of research, but at least one study has found that convicted women are less dangerous as probationers, less likely to violate their probation than men. Women who do violate their probation seldom do so because of another felony (Norland & Mann, 1984). Women's probations are more likely than men's to be revoked because of technical violations, i.e. leaving the jurisdiction, traces of psychoactive substance in the urine, failure to report to probation officer, etc.

Men and women are both likely to find that an intermediate step between incarceration and freedom, like a halfway house, makes the transition to life outside prison more likely to have a successful outcome for the offender and the community (Dowell, Klein, Krichman, 1985).

# Summary

Looking back over the history of women's prisons in the U.S. provides an interesting perspective on the "separate but equal" doctrine. When women have been held together with men in prisons, the conditions often have been disadvantageous for women. When women have developed prisons exclusively for women, they have also perpetrated disadvantages and sexual stereotypes. On one hand, women's prison administrators have to assert their integrity from the system of men's prisons. Women prisoners *do* have different needs than men. This is specifically true with regard to security and programs (Hunter, 1984: 131). Women do not need maximum levels of custody and surveillance; most female criminals are not aggressive or violent. But women do need programs to strengthen family ties and prepare them to make choices as mothers. They are a high priority for corrections.

On the other hand, both women and men need training to prepare them for economic independence (De Costanzo & Valente, 1984: 120). This is another serious priority for corrections. In many cases, it calls for sexual integration of vocational training programs for offenders. Experiences in the history of corrections for women in America have shown that security and programming are compatible in prison. It will be the challenge of the corrections departments of the future to find applications of the doctrine of "separate but equal" that are in the best interests of women and men.

# Notes

1  1984 statistics were provided by the Public Information Officer at Alderson. 1985 statistics were available through the Office of Research, Federal Bureau of Prisons, U.S. Department of Justice, Washington, D.C.

# References

Baunach, P. (1985). *Mothers in prison*. New Brunswick, NJ: Transaction.

Bertram, J. (1982). My real prison is being separated from my children. *Prison MATCH* San Francisco: National Council on Crime and Delinquency.

Bowker, L. (1977). *Prisoner subcultures*. Lexington, MA:D.C. Heath.

Bowker, L. (1981). *Women and crime in America*. New York: Macmillan.

Burkhart, K. (1973). *Women in prison*. New York: Popular Library.

Campbell, C. (1980). *Serving time together*. Fort Worth: Texas Christian University Press.

Campbell, C. (1982). *Shared resources* (The implementation of co-corrections at the Hiland Mountain and Meadow Creek Correctional Centers, Eagle River, Alaska) Report to the Alaska Division of Adult Corrections, July, 1982.

Cavior, H., Hayes, S. & Cavior, N. (1974). Physical attractiveness of female offenders. *Criminal Justice And Behavior*, 1(4), 321-331.

Chandler, E. (1973). *Women in prison*. Indianapolis, IN:Bobbs-Merrill.

Clemmer, D. (1940). *The prison community*. Boston: The Christopher Publishing House.

CONtact, Inc. (1981). Women offenders. Lincoln, NB: *Corrections Compendium*, 5(10) 1-9.

Datesman, S.(1981). Women, crime and drugs. In J. Inciardi (Ed.), *The drugs-crime connection*. Beverly Hills: 1981.

Datesman, S. & Cales, G. (1983). I'm still the same mommy. *The Prison Journal*, 63(2) 142-154.

DeCostanzo, E. & Valente, J. (1984). Designing a corrections continuum for female offenders. *The Prison Journal* 64(1) 120-128.

Dowell, D. , Klein C. & Krichman, C. (1985). Evaluation of a halfway house for women. *Journal Of Criminal Justice*, 13(3) 217-226.

Epperson, D., Hannum, H. & Datwyler, M. (1982). Women incarcerated in 1960, 1970, and 1980. *Criminal Justice And Behavior*, 9(3) 352-363.

Feinman, C.(1986). *Women in the criminal justice system.* New York: Praeger.

Feinman, C. (1983). An historical overview of the treatment of incarcerated women. *The Prison Journal.* 63(2) 12-26.

Flynn, E. (1963). *The Alderson story.* New York: International.

Fox, J. (1984). Women's prison policy,....and the contemporary feminist movement. *The Prison Journal*, 64(1) 15-36.

Freedman, E. (1981). *Their sisters' keepers* Ann Arbor, MG: University of Michigan Press.

Giallombardo, R. (1966). *Society of women.* New York: John Wiley and Sons.

Giallombardo, R. (1966). Social roles in a prison for women. *Social Problems*, 13(3) 269-288.

Gibson, H.E. (1976). Women's prisons: laboratories for penal reform. In, L. Crites (Ed.), *The female offender.* Lexington, MA: D. C. Heath.

Goetting, A. & Howsen, R. (1983). Women in prison: A profile. *The Prison Journal*, 63(2) 27-46.

Haft, M. (1980). Women in prison: Discriminatory practices and some legal solutions. In, S. Datesman & F. Scarpitti (Eds.), *Women, crime and justice.* New York: Oxford.

Haley, K. (1980). Mothers behind bars. In, S. Datesman & F. Scarpitti (Eds.), *Women, crime and justice.* New York: Oxford.

Heffernan, E. (1972). *Making it in prison.* New York: Wiley-Interscience.

Hunter, S. (1984).  Issues and challenges facing women's prisons in the 1980's. *The Prison Journal*, 64(1) 129-135

Kolman, A. (1983).  Support and control patterns of inmate mothers. *The Prison Journal*, 63(2) 155-166.

Kruttschnitt, C.(1981).  Prison codes, inmate solidarity and women. In M. Warren (Ed.), *Comparing female and male offenders*. Beverly Hills, CA:Sage.

Korba Associates, Inc. (1977).  *LEAA phase 1 assessment of coeducational corrections*. Washington, DC: U.S. Dept. of Justice ( National Institute of Law Enforcement and Criminal Justice).

Lindquist, C. (1980).  Prison discipline and the female offender. *Journal Of Offender Counseling Services And Rehabilitation*, 4(4) 305-318.

McGarrell, E. & Flanagan, T. (Eds.), (1984).  Persons under correctional supervision. *Sourcebook of criminal justice statistics—1984, NCJ 96382*. Washington, DC: U.S. Dept. of Justice; U.S. Govt. Printing Office.

McGowan, B. & Blumenthal, K. (1978).  *Why punish the children?* Hackensack, NJ: National Council on Crime and Delinquency.

Mahan, S. (1982).  *Unfit mothers*. Saratoga, CA: R&E Research.

Mahan, S (1984).  Imposition of despair. *Justice Quarterly*, 1(3) 357-383.

Mahan, S (1986).  Doing Time Together. *Corrections Today*, August, 134-142.

Mahan, S. et al. (1987).  *Evaluation of policy for co-corrections*. Federal Bureau of Prisons Research Report, Department of Research, FCI—FW, January, 1986. Washington, DC: American Correctional Association, Forthcoming.

Moyer, I. (1980).  Leadership in a women's prison. *Journal Of Criminal Justice*, 8(4) 233-241.

Moyer, I. (1984).  Deceptions and realities of life in women's prisons. *The Prison Journal*, 24(1) 45-56.

National Advisory Commission on Criminal Justice Standards and Goals (1973). *Task force on corrections*. Washington, DC: U.S. Government Printing Office.

(NCCD) National Council on Crime and Delinquency (1980). *Characteristics of the parole population, 1978*. Washington, DC: U.S. Gov't. Printing Office.

Neto, V. & Bainer, L. (1983). Mother and wife locked up. *The Prison Journal*, 63(2) 124-141.

Norland, S. & Mann, P. (1984) Being troublesome: Women on probation. *Criminal Justice And Behavior*. 11(2) 115-135.

Pollack, J. (1984). Women will be women. *The Prison Journal*, 64(1) 84-89.

Propper, A. (1982). Make-believe families and homosexuality among imprisoned girls. *Criminology*, 20(1) 127-138.

Rafter, N. (1983) Prisons for women, 1790-1800. In M. Tonry & N. Morris (Eds.), *Crime and justice*. Chicago: University of Chicago Press.

Rafter, N. (1985). *Partial justice*. Boston, MA: Northeastern University Press.

Rasche, C. (1975). The female offender as an object of criminological research. In A. Brodsky (Ed.), *The Female Offender*. Beverly Hills, CA: Sage.

Richie-Mann, C. (1984) *Female crime and delinquency*. University, AL: University of Alabama Press.

Roundtree,G., Mohan, B. & Mahaffey, M. (1980) Determinants of female aggression. *International Journal of Offender Therapy And Comparative Criminology*, 24(3) 260-69.

Ryan, T. (1984). *State Of The Art Analysis Of Adult Female Offenders, And Institutional Programs*. Washington, DC: U. S. Dept. of Justice, Natl. Institute for Corrections.

Sargent, J. (1984). The evolution of a stereotype: Paternalism and the female inmate. *The Prison Journal*, 64(1) 37-41.

SchWeber, C. (1980). Pioneers in prison. *Federal Probation*, 44(3) 30-36.

SchWeber, C. (1982). The government's unique experiment in salvaging women criminals, In N. Rafter & E. Stanko (Eds.), *Judge, lawyer, victim, thief.* Boston: Northeastern University Press.

SchWeber, C. (1984). Beauty marks and blemishes: The co ed prison. *The Prison Journal*, 24(1) 3-14.

Shaw, N. (1982). Female patients and the medical profession in jails and prisons. In N. Rafter & E. Stanko (Eds.), *Judge, lawyer, victim, thief.* Boston:NorthEastern Univ. Press.

Ward, D. & Kassebaum, G. (1965). *Women's prison*, Chicago: Aldine.

VanWormer, K. & Bates, F. (1979). A study of leadership roles in an Alabama prison for women. *Human Relations*, 32(9) 793-801.

Wheeler, M. (1974). The current status of women in prisons. *Criminal Justice and Behavior*, 1(4) 374-380.

Wheeler, S. (1961). Socialization in correctional communities. *American Sociological Review*, 26(1) 697-706.

Zingraff, M. (1980). Inmate assimilation of male and female delinquents. *Criminal Justice and Behavior*, 7(3) 275-292.

# 5

# "Keeping Women In Their Place:" Incest, Rape, Battering, and Harassment*

## Introduction

The four crimes which are covered in this chapter have existed from earliest times. The myths about them have their origins in our most honored literary traditions.

Here are some examples:

INCEST:   (From The Old Testament, Book of Genesis 19:30-38)

*And they made their father drink wine that night: and the
firstborn went in, and lay with her father; and he
perceived not when she lay down, nor when she arose.
And it came to pass on the morrow, that the firstborn said
unto the younger, Behold, I lay yesternight with my father:
let us make him drink wine this night also; and go thou
in and lie with him, that we may preserve seed of our father.*

*And they made their father drink wine that night also: and
the younger arose, and lay with him; and he perceived not
when she lay down, nor when she arose.
Thus were both the daughters of Lot with child by their father.*

RAPE:   (From The Old Testament, Book of Judges, 19:22-24)

*The men of the city, base fellows, beset the
house round about, beating on the door; and they said to the*

*old man, the master of the house, 'Bring out the man who came
into your house, that we may know him.' And the man, the
master of the house, went out to them and said to them, 'No
my brethren, do not act so wickedly...here are my virgin
daughter and his concubine; let me bring them out now.
Ravish them and do with them what seems good to you; but
against this man do not do so vile a thing.'*

BATTERING:     (From Shakespeare, The Taming of The
               Shrew, Act IV: Scene I, Petruchio's
               Speech)

*Thus have I politicly begun my reign,
And 'tis my hope to end successfully.
And till she stoop, she must not be full-gorg'd,
For then she never looks upon her lure.
Another way I have to man my haggard,
To make her come, and know her keeper's call,
That is, to watch her, as we watch those kites
That bate, and beat, and will not be obedient.
She eat no meat today, nor none shall eat;
Last night she slept not, nor to-night she shall not;
As with the meat, some underserved fault
I'll find about the making of the bed;
And here I'll fling the pillow, there the bolster,
This way the coverlet, another way the sheets:—
Ay, and amid this hurly, I intend
That all is done in reverend care of her;
And in conclusion she shall watch all night:
And if she chance to nod, I'll rail and brawl,
And with the clamour keep her still awake.
This is the way to kill a wife with kindness:
And thus I'll curb her mad and headstrong humour.
He that knows better how to tame a shrew,
Now let him speak; 'tis charity to show.*

HARASSMENT:  (From Beyond Good and Evil, by Friedrich
             Nietzsche)

*To go wrong on the fundamental problem of 'man and
woman,'...to dream perhaps of equal rights, equal
education, equal claims and obligations—that is*

*a TYPICAL sign of shallowness, and a thinker who has
proved shallow in this dangerous place...may be considered
altogether suspicious,...probably he will be too "short"
for all fundamental problems of life, of the life yet to
come, too, and incapable of attaining ANY depth...
woman now aspires to the economic and legal self-
reliance of a clerk: "woman as clerk" is inscribed on the
gate to the modern society that is taking shape now. As
she thus takes possession of new rights, aspires to become
"master" and writes the "progress" of woman upon her
standards and banners, the opposite development is taking
place with terrible clarity: woman is retrogressing.*

## The Victimization of Women

When it comes to what the FBI calls "serious crime," women do not appear to be victimized as much as men by crimes and criminals in America. Men are far more likely to be the victims of reported assaults and murders than women. Yet, women in America live with a much greater fear of being criminally victimized than men. The difference is, females are much more likely to be victimized by a male with whom they have a personal relationship. Because of the differences in the ways in which women are victimized, they are not as likely to report their experiences to the police. And because of the values and beliefs about the crimes in which females are usually victimized, their stories may be discredited and their cases dismissed. In fact, female victims are sometimes blamed for the crime themselves.

Four different types of offenses against women provide excellent examples of the ways women are likely to be victimized by men in personal relationships: incest, rape, battering, and sexual harassment in the work place. Of course there are male victims of these crimes, too. But, these are four crimes for which the reports of female victims far outnumber those of male victims, by even as much as 100 to one. The drastic differences are reported in every survey, and in every jurisdiction.

These crimes are all drastically underreported, too. It is also interesting that there are persistent public misunderstandings about all four of these crimes which are known as "myths." The myths are the same for all four, even though the context and circumstances may be drastically different. The most significant characteristic that these four different types of crimes have in common, though, is their impact on social life. Each one of them serves the same purpose: keeping women in their place.

# The Myths

**Myth Number One**—*She likes it...secretly wants it.*

This first myth about women victims negates the harm of the crime and denies the legitimacy of the victim. There are variations of the idea which are specifically related to each of the four crimes, but the central theme remains the same.

Incest—It doesn't really hurt anyone.

Rape—Most women have rape fantasies, and would like to live them out.

Battering—Some women like to be beaten.

Harassment—Most successful women trade sexual favors for opportunities.

**Myth Number Two**—*She asked for it... 'no' means 'yes'.*

The second set of myths about women victims also denies the legitimacy of the victims. It introduces the idea of "victim precipitation," and puts the burden of proof on the victim to show, not only that the crime happened, but also that her own behavior was within the bounds of propriety. Just what those bounds are, though, is certainly far from clear. Many victims report that their father, boyfriend, husband or boss forced his sexuality on them to teach them a lesson, saying, "I'll show you, you're not TOO GOOD."

Incest—She was very precocious.

Rape—She was in the wrong place at the wrong time. She asked for it by the way she was dressed, or going out with that guy, or hitchhiking, or by getting too drunk.

Battering—She was nagging, whoring or lazy.

Harassment—She had a "bad reputation."

**Myth Number Three**—*Men can't help themselves.*
This type of myth denies the responsibility of the offender. According to this way of thinking, any reasonable man would certainly have acted in a similar way when confronted by such unreasonable provocation.

Incest—He wasn't being satisfied by his wife.

Rape—He felt an irresistible impulse.

Battering—He had to prove he was a man.

Harassment—She led him into it.

**Myth Number Four**—*Any man who would commit _____ must be crazy.*
This set of myths distorts the true nature of these crimes, because it presents the offender in the wrong light. Instead of being depicted as a father, husband, boyfriend or boss, the offender is portrayed as a monster. Actually, the criminal in these four kinds of crime is simply acting out the most extreme forms of typical relationships between men and women in American society. Yet females are thought to need protection from mad men on the dark streets at night, not at home in the bedroom, or in the office where they work. This myth legitimizes an image of the offender as a marginal man, and makes it difficult to prosecute a powerful man, no matter what the evidence against him may be.

Incest—Strangers (Pedophiliacs) are kidnapping children.

Rape—Rapist are insane, sexual psychopaths.

Battering—He only does it when he's drunk.

Harassment—Only perverts and lechers would really "take advantage" of women who can't say no.

**Myth Number Five**—*It is rare and happens to the 'lower classes'.*
No tabulation of the amount of these four crimes can really be accurate, because of the secrecy and social stigma involved with them. From time to time there have been campaigns to make the public aware of their wide-spread nature. However, the campaigns are often about crimes which are not common or deal with actions that are really extreme. The

rest of the sexual exploitation and abuse of females often goes unreported and unremarked.

Incest—It is a strict taboo.

Rape—Only a few, careless women are raped.

Battering—It only happens in poor families with social problems.

Harassment—Serious sexual molesting in the work world is uncommon, mostly it's a joke.

Although there are common elements in these four crimes, there are certainly differences between them, too. Because of their differences, a separate analysis is needed for each of the four types of victimization. However, in order to keep the similarities in mind, the same framework has been used for studying all four of the crimes in this chapter. For a personal perspective, the roles and relationships of the victims have been included. These four social problems have also been explained from a cultural standpoint. The legal issues involved in each of these four crimes have been explored, too. Finally, social policies regarding each of these four crimes have been evaluated as they relate to victims, offenders and situations which are criminogenic. In general, policies which have the goal of correcting crime-prone situations, rather than victims or offenders, have the most far-reaching impact for victims and potential victims.

Each section in this chapter ends with a brief description of a program designed to address the four types of victimization of women. The programs described are short range and limited attempts to deal with the crimes. These program descriptions are meant to give you an idea about "typical" organizations' efforts to meet the significant social problems these four crimes present.

## Incest

### *Roles and Relationships—Father Dominant Patriarch*

Incest occurs in families from all socio-economic classes and occupational groups. But there is one common element found in families where incest is reported, that is a dominant, patriarchal father figure. This man intends to control his family with an iron hand and sees the family members as "his" to use as he sees fit. Incestuous fathers seldom have criminal records, often are seen as upstanding members of the community, likely to be conservative and traditional in lifestyle and beliefs. Maybe this father is insecure and anxious about his sexuality underneath his exterior role as patriarch. If so, he is inept at dealing with weakness and unlikely to express his feelings to others.

In extreme cases, the incestuous father rapes his daughter, using force if necessary. In most cases, the father figure uses less drastic measures of imposing his sexuality on his child.

Fondling, exhibitionism, and oral sexual activities are much more common than genital penetration. The offender is not usually concerned with the child's feelings or needs; his own gratification is his only interest in incest. Often the father initiates his daughter into incest by rewards and by playing on her affection for him. Later, when the little girl resists, he may turn to force and threat to get his way. In most reported cases, the sexual contact has persisted over many years. In some cases, the father uses more than one of his daughters as a sex object, beginning with the oldest and taking advantage of the younger ones as they mature.

It is common in the isolated nuclear family of patriarchal modern society for the dominant father figure to have absolute power. It is a position which invites absolute corruption. Incest is one of the forms that corruption takes.

## *The Cultural Signs — Sexual Objectification*

Incest is a pervasive problem in our patriarchal modern society. It is in evidence in an almost taken-for-granted aspect of male-female relationships. The relationship between a daughter and a father is often the first and most profound female/male relationship experienced by a female. In a society where incest is common, a young female learns what to expect in relationships between the sexes in the family. She learns early on that she can get what she wants from dominant males by flattering them, exciting them, titillating them, manipulating them. She has learned that from her father. She has also learned that dominant males will treat her like property, an object to satisfy their own needs. So she has learned sexual objectification from both sides — using men, and being used by them.

For the male, sexual objectification begins at home, too. He learns that he must control others to prove his maleness, and that females are servants to males. Sexual objectification provides a fundamental conflict on which the battle of the sexes is founded. It begins early, and generally from the onset the female is at a disadvantage. By exerting dominance over his daughter, and using her for his own selfish desires, an incestuous father is preparing this female child to assume her traditional, subservient role in social life in general and in the family in particular. It is not a coincidence that victims of incest are more likely than other females to experience repeated sexual exploitation and oppression throughout their lives.

## The Law — Testimony of the Victims

There are rarely any witnesses to incest except for the victim herself. But there are two issues that inevitably arise when the evidence in a court case is presented by a child: witness protection and credibility of testimony. It is presumed that the courtroom is a traumatic place for a child, that being questioned is frightening, and that publicity is damaging for a young person who has already been victimized. It is also presumed that children are not really aware of the difference between truth and lying, and that they do not really understand everything they experience or testify as clearly and explicitly as an adult. The presumptions of victim harm and lack of reliability are relevant to the testimony in all four of the crimes covered in this section. The law which enforces the incest taboo must consider ways to provide protection for the victims, and enhance their credibility as witnesses.

Recently there have been legal efforts in many jurisdictions to accept pre-recorded videotaped testimony from children about their accusations of molesting as evidence in criminal trials. These efforts have been attempts to keep the child victim from experiencing the traumatic effects of testifying in open court. However, some procedures sacrifice due process because they make it impossible for the accused to cross-examine the witnesses against him. Legal efforts would be better served if they were directed toward humanizing the court process in order to protect witnesses and increase the credibility of testimony. Harsh treatment of offenders in court, and public outrage about child molesters may simply perpetuate the myth that child molesters are monsters, and will mean fewer charges will be brought against those who are actually molesting children in their own families.

## Incest Policy: Victim

Solutions for the social problem of incest have often been aimed at the victim rather than the offender. Programs for schools, the mass media, and for social groups have emphasized the idea that children have autonomy over their own bodies. It is hoped that potential victims will not be so easily seduced or subdued if they understand about sexual oppression and have already practiced saying "no." Unfortunately, many of these presentations present an image of the offender as a stranger, when it is more likely that offenders are men who are known to the child victim.

The message to children in some of the incest prevention programs is that they must report the offender, and that they can trust the authorities to protect them from him afterward. Of course, reporting is easier for victims of sexual molesting by strangers than for victims of incest. Children who have learned to distrust their own fathers are likely to find it hard to trust the authorities, too. The incest relationship is emotional and embarrassing for the victim, usually a well kept secret.

Furthermore, the offender (fearing exposure) has probably threatened the child victim with some great harm if she tells anybody about their relationship. Being her father, the offender is in a very good position to know what would most frighten the victim, and is often around to remind her of the threat, too. So it is doubtful that the victim awareness approach to incest prevention is having much impact on the problem.

## Incest Policy: Offender

Incest intervention programs aimed at offenders do claim success, at least on a limited scale. The usual scenario involves an offender who is reported for the crime, and must be forced to give up his idea that "I'm not hurting anyone." After facing prosecution, the offender may benefit from court-ordered treatment.

The most successful therapy involves others who are also overcoming the same incestuous behavior. Self-help groups are solutions for offenders which do not cost anything, and which have a positive impact on those who participate. The idea is that the best person to provide treatment for bad habits is someone who has overcome the habit. The concept has proved useful in the treatment of alcoholics, drug addicts, and compulsive eaters as well as child molesters.

## Incest Policy: Situation

Real prevention of incest must be aimed more at structural conditions than individuals. Reorganizing patriarchal families to include group decision making and to emphasize the autonomy of the individual makes incest less likely. Preventing incest also depends on providing potential molesters with more constructive ways of expressing emotions. That means a revision of the "John Wayne" image of males as dominant, unexpressive and violence prone. Changes in male sex roles will mean changes in female sex roles and family roles as cultural adjustments and readjustments follow.

*Dealing with the problems—"A Training Curriculum"*

In 1981, the Vermont Department of Social and Rehabilitative Services developed a training curriculum for human services professionals to prepare them for intervention in incestuous families. The course is divided into seven sessions which may be given in two days of intensive classes or combinations of two and three hour classes. The topics covered in the seven sessions are: clarifying one's own values about incest, the dynamics of the incestuous family, the initial interview with the victim, the development of an intervention plan, the team approach to intervention and networking. Materials include: books, articles, films and videos.

From: <u>Intervention with Incestuous Families</u> by A.L. Dorwaldt, (1983). Rockville, MD: NIJ/NJCRS, Box 6000.

# Rape

## *The Roles—Lover as Aggressor in Sexual Matters*

If incest is simply the extreme form of the father/daughter relationship in a patriarchal society, then it follows that rape is the extreme of the lover relationship in patriarchy. Where men are automatically designated aggressors in sexual matters, extremes of aggression can be expected. In our culture the role of sexual aggressor has a violent component. Sex and violence are linked in lurid films, literature, music videos, and certainly they are also linked in the lives of many men and women. Violence is more likely to lead to sexual arousal in men than in women, though, because it is aggressive and consistent with the role of sexual master which is considered appropriate for the male.

What happens to females who assert control over their own sexuality? What about women who sell their sexuality, for example, prostitutes? In fact, women who are prostitutes are much more likely to be the victims of aggressive and violent sexual imposition than other women, and much less likely to be treated as legitimate victims. A man who rapes a prostitute stands little chance of being charged for the crime, and almost no chance of being convicted. You might say that it is one of the occupational hazards for prostitutes that they can be raped with impunity.

Unlike prostitutes, the "legitimate" victim of rape is one who is likely to report the crime to the police, and likely to be treated as a credible witness.

What are the characteristics of "legitimate" victims? Females who are married or virginal, living with their families, white, respectable, and who suffer violence from a stranger are much more likely to be taken seriously as rape victims. On the other hand, those who are divorced or single, living alone, black and who are overcome by a man with whom they are acquainted are much less likely to be thought of as "legitimate" victims.

On the other hand, a "legitimate" offender is more likely to be arrested and convicted for rape. What are the characteristics of "legitimate" offenders? Usually, males who are single or divorced, under or unemployed, black and who have criminal histories are charged and convicted of rape. White, married, professional men are seldom considered "legitimate" rapists. They are protected by the myths which picture rapists as deviants and sexual psychopaths.

There are three categories of rapists, according to A.N. Groth, who studied offenders extensively. He designated the types of rapists as: power, anger and sadistic rapists. Power rapists can be identified by their attempts to dominate their victims and humiliate them. Power rapists may have the delusion that they will gain their victim's undying devotion by subduing her sexually. They will use force and threat, but somehow they must maintain the illusion that the victim really wants their sexual attention, that she 'asked for it.' Anger rapists have a more deep-seated hostility for females. They prefer to punish their victims. They are willing to resort to force and have no illusion about a relationship between themselves and the victim. In fact, extreme resistance from the victim may be arousing to the angry rapist. He may enjoy his victim's suffering and cries of pain. The most extreme rapist is a sadistic rapist who has carried the anger rape to its ultimate horror. Although sadistic rapists only make up a small part of the population of rape offenders, they attain wide notoriety for the heinous nature of their crimes. Violent, sadistic rapes are the prototypical crimes which strike fear in women's hearts. However, women are much more likely to be involved in a power rape, assaulted by a man they know.

## Cultural Signs — Pornography

Aggressive sexuality against women is an integral part of male/female relationships in modern U.S. social life. Evidence for the widespread value placed on dominating women sexually is made explicit in pornographic magazines marketed to men. Rape or sexual imposition is a common theme in pornographic films and literature. Disrespect for women and humiliation is also common.

The link between buying pornographic materials and committing rape may not be a direct one. Not all rapists are pornography fans, and not all fans of pornography commit rape, either. But there is, at the least, an indirect link between the popularity of materials which encourage dominating and humiliating females and the prevalence of crimes which succeed in doing just that. Pornography directly victimizes women when it sexually objectifies them, and encourages masochism and violence.

Pornography can be defined as the graphic depiction of sexual coercion, imposition or exploitation (other explicit sexual materials being designated as erotica). From that perspective, sexual materials involving children are pornographic regardless of their content. Though there is public outrage and cries for vengeance whenever an offender is charged for child pornography, the market for pornographic materials involving children equals millions of dollars. The vast demand for "kiddie porn" means that despite age old taboos, the sexual exploitation of children continues.

## The Law—Consent; Penetration

The legal definition of rape varies from jurisdiction to jurisdiction. Probably the most commonly cited definition comes from the FBI's *Uniform Crime Reports*: "The carnal knowledge of a female forcibly and against her will." This definition contains two of the legal elements which are so problematic where rape is concerned. In the first place there is the element of consent, which implies that the burden of proof rests with the victim to show that the sexual imposition was against her will. The defense may try to show that the victim has lost the right of consent over her sexuality because of her "bad reputation." In a few states, "rape shield laws" protect the victim from the disclosure of her sexual history in court. But the inclusion of sexual history is especially significant, if the sexual history includes past sexual relations with the offender. It is implied that having sex with a man once gives him the right to demand sexual relations indefinitely thereafter. For the victim it implies that she lost the right to refuse to have sex with a man the first time she consented.

Most prosecutors demand proof of lack of consent before they take a rape case to court. That demand has often meant that resistance must be demonstrated. In some cases, the victim is not taken seriously unless she is bruised and beaten, and some rape victims feel compelled to resist a rapist regardless of the threat. For some victims, their active resistance meant death or at least serious injury. Although women may realize that to resist a rapist with a weapon or to fight back against an angry rapist who has threatened to kill them is suicidal, they may find that unless they fight their attacker and possibly provoke him into harming them, they will not be believed.

The second legal element contained in the FBI definition is *penetration*. Medical evidence is generally required to prove that carnal knowledge of the female took place. Usually the medical tests are meant to determine if there is trauma to the vagina or sperm present. It is difficult to sustain a charge of rape without medical confirmation. Victims who bathe before seeing authorities may not have a chance of proving they were raped. There are also reports from some victims that the medical examination proved to be as traumatic as the rape. Even when emergency room procedures are concerned and humane, many times the victim must foot the bill to provide the legal evidence of penetration.

The legal demand for proof of penetration derives from a false image of the rapist as a virile male unable to contain his overwhelming sexual drive. The image of the act of rape as male penile insertion fulfilling the rapist's creative need to propagate and procreate is far from the reality experienced by most rape victims. Rather than an overwhelming impulse, rape is likely to be planned in advance. In reality, many rapists have feelings of inferiority and sexual impotency. It is likely that they may be unable to sustain an erection, and ejaculation inside the vagina is certainly only one of many alternatives. Sexual impositions may just as likely involve oral sex and not result in evidence of vaginal trauma or semen.

Many jurisdictions have introduced reforms in their laws regarding rape which are intended to protect victims and more effectively prosecute offenders with the outcome of more convictions and longer sentences for rapists. As they have worked out, many of the reforms have neither protected victims nor punished offenders. For one reason or another, the conviction rate of rapists remains low, the numbers of solved cases is also low and the victims still find that treatment in the system of justice is often as terrible as the rape. The harsh treatment of the victim inside the system has been known as secondary victimization. It is relevant for victims of all four of the crimes of sexual exploitation that are discussed in this chapter.

The following is a system of categorization for types of rape which clarifies all of the elements involved, without putting the burden of proof on the victim about the validity of her claims about the crime:

### Degrees of Rape

first    aggravated—aggravated assault with bodily harm
         and/or use of weapon

second   high—kidnapping and/or illegal entry in order to
         commit a sexual attack

third        serious—penetration and/or invasion of person

fourth       simple—sexual imposition and threats of sexual
             imposition and/or invasion of privacy

The classification of first through fourth degrees of rape which is spelled out above puts all of the aspects of sexual imposition in place. Using this schema, consent and penetration are only at issue in serious and simple rapes.    In the higher degrees of rape, felonies related to the crime compound its significance. The highest degree of all is death as the result of a sexual attack, which is murder not rape, and  treated accordingly. In this categorization, sexual assault is the term used for second degree rape or for aggravated rape. So the terms rape and sexual assault cannot really be used interchangeably as they have been in many other places.

According to this system, rape is thought of as sexual imposition and coercion to impose sexuality. This definition is much broader than the one used by the FBI. If we perceive rape this way, according to Russell, there may be as high as a 26% probability that women living in some American cities will fall victim to serious rape at some time in their lives. If the types of sexual impositions listed above as simple rapes are included, there is a 46% probability that women living in urban areas in the U.S. will become victims. For young women and women living alone the probabilities are even higher.   There is no doubt that the actual number of rapes, even according to the FBI's limited definition, is much greater than the 87,340 reported by the police in the Uniform Crime Reports for 1985.

## *Rape Policy:  Victim*

Campaigns to put an end to rape frequently focus on victim preparedness. Some of the campaigns focus on security devices and others emphasize having a suspicious attitude and extreme caution. Unwittingly, those who propose such measures are recommending that women live in prisons of their own making.   Still other rape prevention strategies encourage self defense training and preparation for resistance. The real question is whether or not the rape prevention measures enhance the life of the victim, or if, in fact, victim preparedness really means that women must live with constant fear and restrict their personal freedom in order to keep from being raped.

A second type of effort against rape which is focused on victims is the rape crisis center. These programs sprang up all over the country during the 1970s, with hot lines and victim advocates to help the victim overcome the trauma. Unfortunately, cutbacks in the human services during the 1980s have seriously reduced the usefulness of many of the rape crisis programs. Most of them are operating with severely restricted budgets and some do not have the funds to staff their programs or provide any real crisis-intervention services. Although rape crisis centers may provide care and concern for victims, they are not usually able to handle programs that are aimed at prevention.

## Rape Policy:  Offenders

A different approach to rape prevention is aimed at potential offenders rather than victims. The basis for rape is found in the rapists' negative attitudes and illusions about females, so it makes sense to direct prevention efforts at the relationships between males and females. Although the goal for the programs is reforming males' potentially violent attitudes before they can manifest, the efforts must also involve females. In this type of training boys and girls relate as equals and develop intersexual relationships of trust and co-operation that do not involve sexuality. Men and women are also trained to relate as equals at work, recreation, and in every other aspect of life.

Men who have already manifested violent attitudes toward women are given relationship training involving women therapists and a female-centered approach. They are provided opportunities to see rape from the point of view of the victim,  to experience one-to-one interaction with females as equals, and to discuss their feelings with other men who are also overcoming the desire to harm women.

## Rape Policy:  Situation

Efforts to prevent rape at the societal level include educational programs to promote rape awareness, civic measures including better lighting and transportation systems, and criminal procedures to more strictly enforce the laws against rape. In some cases civil procedures have been filed against third parties in rape cases. For instance, a landlord might be sued for negligence if his property is unsafe and a rape takes place there. A university might be sued if dark and unsavory conditions on campus prove hazardous, or an employer could be sued if working conditions are dangerous.  Legal remedies provide potential rape victims the same protection that is afforded to other tenants, students and employees, and the right to expect to be secure from the threat of bodily harm during the course of their everyday lives.

*Dealing With the Problem — Rape Prevention Program*

Since 1972, the Department of Public Safety at Florida State University (Tallahassee, FL) has been implementing a rape awareness program for university women.  Presentations are held in residence halls, and academic classes, and before other campus and community groups.  The multimedia presentations offers suggestions for rape prevention and reviews the criminal justice system response to a rape victim.   Community involvement has helped to make the rape prevention program a successful one, with a continued low number of reported rapes on university property.

From: Rape prevention program at Florida State University by J.D. Sewell (1981). in <u>Campus Law Enforcement Journal</u>, 11(3), 26-29.

# Battering

## *The Roles — Spouse Achieving Power Over His Property*

There is a third type of victimization which is an extreme form of an ordinary relationship between a man and woman in the U.S.  When men beat their female roommates, spouses, wives or partners, they are acting out the conditions of the marriage contract in traditional patriarchal society.  As the head of the family, the patriarchal authority figure had the right to control the members as a sovereign over his domain.  Although wife beating was never exactly approved, it was thought necessary and even desirable from time to time, "to teach her a lesson."

It may be logical to assume that as the harsh, rigid structures of the traditional family give way in modern life, the instances of wife beating will decline.  However, social change is never unidimensional.  There may even be an increase of violence in the present generation's families if male authority figures feel threatened by increasing freedom and opportunities for females.  For example, in situations where the woman is economically more successful than her male partner, he may resort to violence for control since  he has lost other sources of power.  As occupational opportunities and social supports for independence among women in our culture continue to grow, females still remain emotionally dependent on males and potential victims of abuse from the men they love.

## *The Cultural Sign — Value on Violence*

Many researchers have documented that spouse abuse is an intergenerational familial pattern. That means that children learn it from their parents. More specifically, boys learn it from their fathers. Apparently, girls learn how to be victims the same way. Couples involved in domestic violence often report that they first witnessed it as very young children.

Many times, the authority figure administers violence in the name of discipline. Children learn that the large prey on the small, the strong on the weak. Perhaps they look forward to the day when they will be big enough and strong enough to use violence themselves. They can see that violence is a useful strategy for their father; he gets what he wants from the family after a violent episode, at least in the short run. In the long run, the authoritarian father gets fear and loathing in return for his violence, but he may never perceive the connection.

In other words, cultural violence is a cycle that must be broken at its deepest level, in the family. The young male learns to use violence as a viable solution for his problems, and the young female learns to expect to be abused. Later the familial lesson is reinforced time and again in a myriad of messages which promote violence as a strategy for handling problems. Some examples: government threats of war, police harassment, movie heroes like "Dirty Harry," aggressive sports, popular support for capital punishment, and even the spectacular public interest in crimes of passion.

## *The Law — Criminal and Civil Procedures*

The first contact a battered woman has with the authorities is likely to involve the police. Maybe the victim has called 911 for help, or perhaps the neighbors called to report a disturbance. But when the police show up at the scene of domestic violence, they may be very unwilling participants in the drama. Police officers know that a domestic disturbance is one of the situations which is most likely to lead to injury for them, and realize that the potential for danger is high. Police departments vary in the policies they effect to handle domestic violence, but their options vary along three lines: mediation, civil action, or criminal procedures.

The police may choose to deal with the violence as a social problem rather than a crime. In some jurisdictions, officers are advised to try to act as mediators, but when logic fails, to separate the combatants temporarily. This policy sometimes means no more than, "a ride around the block to cool off," for the batterer, or at worst a night in jail before he returns home more angry than ever. Most police officers report that their first response to a domestic disturbance is to try to talk to the couple and reason with them until the situation is calm. It is no wonder that most battered women who report their victimization to the police report dissatisfaction with the way their problem was handled. The numbers of serious injuries which result from domestic violence despite repeated calls to the police demonstrates the futility of this approach.

In other jurisdictions, police may be trained to suggest civil remedies for victims of spouse abuse. Most often the wife is told to seek an injunction in which the court demands that the offender stay away from her. Such "protection orders" are seldom successful in stopping the abuse. In some cases, the civil injunction prevents the assailant from leaving town, so victims report that the civil proceedings may actually prolong the abuse. Other civil remedies such as fines for offenders or payment of damages to the victim have not been widely applied in cases of domestic violence. However, these remedies may prove to be significant in alleviating the problem of economic dependency for wives trapped in abuse because they have no means of support.

The last legal resort is criminal prosecution for the offender. Usually this alternative is pursued too late, after the wife has been seriously injured or killed. But police and prosecutors in the U.S. believe that wives will not be reliable as witnesses when the case comes up in court. A battered wife is not expected to follow through on a complaint; she is thought to be very likely to drop the charges and make peace with her abuser. Whether or not to pursue criminal proceedings against a wife batterer is the decision of the local prosecutor. Many prosecutors have reportedly issued policies for police officers to dismiss all cases of domestic violence because "they do not hold up in court." Hence police are often reluctant to arrest a wife abuser knowing that the case will never be heard.

A large proportion of all the murders in the U.S. are the result of domestic violence. Among all female murder victims in 1985, 30% were slain by husbands or boyfriends. Just 6% of male victims were slain by wives or girl friends. Nevertheless, too many women eventually fight back against men who have abused them and end up killing their own husbands. The statistics point out the seriousness of the problem of wife abuse, along with the failure of present legal efforts for handling the problem.

## Battering Policy: Victims

One of the most popular measures to handle the problem of wife abuse has been to provide temporary shelters for the victim and her children. Shelters for battered women opened in most cities in the U.S. during the 1970s. The concept was significant because it signaled awakening public concern for abused wives. But the number of women who have actually received the services of a shelter is very small, compared to all the women who need them. In most cities, facilities hold less than 100 families, yet more than 100 domestic disturbances are reported to the police every weekend. Battered wives are forced to turn to family, friends and even in-laws for support. In some cases, the family including the in-laws refuses to help, or cannot. In other cases, the victim has no one to whom she can turn.

Battered wives who are able to move into a shelter temporarily can benefit from the respite from violence in many ways. Counselors can provide crisis intervention to assist the victims in changing their lives and putting a stop to the abuse.

Children can also be given counseling while they are staying in the shelter, and physical needs can be attended. But there is no denying that these are temporary benefits, and no solution.

## *Battering Policy: Offenders*

Another approach to wife battering involves the batterer instead of the victim. It is important to an offender-directed approach that the wife must leave the husband, or put him out of the house. Unless the abuser realizes that he will lose his wife and family, there is little hope of convincing him to stop battering them. After the shock of losing his family, an offender may be a good candidate for treatment.

The key to treatment for wife battering is alleviating jealousy and possessiveness in the relationship between the abuser and his spouse. Dealing with abusers is a beginning. More significant is developing an understanding of the dysfunction of jealousy in human relations. Jealousy is part of the sexual objectification of women. Possessiveness is the signal that a woman is being treated like property. Extreme jealousy from a male lover is a very dangerous and glaring sign of trouble ahead in a relationship.

## *Battering Policy: Situation*

The most important efforts to end domestic violence are aimed at the children. Since most men learned to abuse their families as small boys watching their fathers, it is reasonable to expect that little boys are still learning those violent lessons today. But it is not inevitable that they must some day act out their violent impulses on their wives as a lesson for the next generation of children. Instead, children today can learn non-violent ways of handling conflict, non-aggressive ways of handling stress, and the negative, long-term effects of acting out violently. But as long as the cultural messages encouraging violence bombard children from every side, lessons in non-violence may not have much effect.

### Dealing With the Problem—The Military Family

*The Military Family* was written primarily for professional therapists working with military families. Over 55% of active duty personnel are 30 years old or younger; this is an age group that is most likely to engage in family violence. The military family is also removed from the support system of the extended family which makes them more prone to family violence. The military requires reporting any known case of domestic violence, and can order the husband into evaluation and treatment. Coercion and initial lack of motivation do not preclude successful therapy. This is consistent with military studies that show draftees do better than volunteers. Since treatment is difficult, real solutions are primarily preventive and educational. Elements of successful programs are: effective sanctions, mental health treatment, communications skills training, constructive coping with stress and frustration, provision of an nonviolent sociopolitical environment, and less violent contexts for the mass media.

From: The Military Family by Florence W. Ridemour & Richard I. Ridemour, (1984). New York: The Guilford Press.

# Sexual Harassment in the Workplace

## The Role—Boss Taking the Privileges to Which He Is Due

Ever since the relationship of male master and female servant developed in society, there has been a persistent understanding that the dominant male will, from time to time, take sexual "liberties" with the subordinate female. It is also commonly assumed that whenever possible the inferior female will use her sexuality to gain privileges from the superior male. The sexual objectification that begins with an incestuous family finds its culmination in sexual harassment in the workplace.

Women may find that they are seen as ornaments in the labor market rather than real contenders for control. Some females are hired more for their appearances than their skills; others find that physical attractiveness is a condition for employment regardless of their training or experience.

In the majority of cases the harassment is subtle, passed off as humor or complimentary. The sexual innuendos reinforce the powerful employer by embarrassing and objectifying the women who work for him. In other cases, the female employee learns that the harassment is not so subtle. She may find she is not considered for a promotion because of her sex. She may be excluded from important all-male meetings, face discrimination in work assignments, and seldom be given credit for her accomplishments. Even worse, a surprising number of women in the labor force experience sexual impositions and even assaults from their employers.

## *The Cultural Sign—The Economic Position of Women*

Sexual harassment in the work place is more than just embarrassing and belittling for female employees. It serves to perpetuate economic inferiority for women in the U.S. Sexual harassment not only perpetuates the sexist ideas of powerful men, it reinforces the poor self image of powerless women. It helps to maintain the status quo as far as women are concerned because it builds obstacles to success and power for females while discouraging them from trying to overcome the obstacles they encounter. Instead, women are encouraged to devote themselves to their appearances rather than to creating value in the labor market.

## *The Law—Losses and Gains*

Although some women have won law suits against men who harassed them at work, the decisions have not clearly favored the victim. At best, the outcomes of attempts to gain remedies in court for sexual harassment have been limited. Many wins for female victims in lower courts have been overturned in appeals to higher courts.

Probably the most common way of handling complaints of sexual harassment is through internal affairs regulatory policies from within the organization. Sometimes administrative hearings result in dismissal or transfer for the harasser. But many women complain that the internal affairs procedure was not really fact finding, and that they were not satisfied with the way their cases were treated. Sometimes the offender is not sanctioned at all, and after the hearing the female employee may face more harassment instead of less.

When sexual harassment is litigated as a civil suit, the court may demand damages from the organization, not just from the offending male. That threat may lead companies to issue strict policies against sexual harassment. However, court action has little effect on the subtle, insidious sexual harassment which may be the most damaging of all.

Criminal prosecution of sexual harassers is very rare, although simple and even serious rape in the work place is not that rare according to victims' self reports. Females in low-status, service related occupations report the most frequent and serious harassment of all. These are the very ones who are most dependent on their employment for survival, and who are least likely to be taken seriously as legitimate victims.

## Sexual Harassment Policy:  Victim

The first step in preventing sexual harassment in the work place has been taken by victims who refused to submit to being objectified.  There have been countless examples of female victims in recent years who have begun formal proceedings against employers for belittling them, discriminating against them or imposing sexuality on them.   Such proceedings may have had mixed returns for the victims involved, but they have increased public awareness of the problem, and made sexual harassment less acceptable.  In the future, these kinds of open hearings may actually make it less likely that potential victims will accept sexual harassments as a necessary aspect of employment.   Others may be more likely to confront their harassers when they know that they are not alone.

Exposure of cases of sexual harassment may also discourage future offenders. If other men in positions of power are publicly sanctioned for taking advantage of their female employees' positions of powerlessness, a potential harasser may reconsider his treatment of his employees.

## Sexual Harassment Policy:  Offender

Significant prevention of sexual harassment must be based on real changes in the domain of power.  Stopping the abuse depends on men.  It is important that men who are concerned about human rights confront their male colleagues and friends when they hear about sexual exploitation. Laughing at sexist remarks, or even silence, can easily be construed as encouragement.   Organizations which are concerned about sexual harassment have given workshops and seminars for all employees to inform them of the legal mandate for equal policies and equal treatment for females.  These sessions may also include experiences and role playing to help males understand the effects of sexual harassment on female victims.

## Sexual Harassment Policy:  Situation

The offense of sexual harassment is important for maintaining male supremacy in the labor market.  It must be eliminated through increased opportunities for women to achieve power in the economic realm. As more and more women gain positions of control and authority, the environments for sexual harassment of females will eventually evaporate. However, during the time of transition and change, sexual harassment may become an even greater problem. Some men in power may resist change and feel threatened by the encroachment of successful females, and they may retaliate with the age old strategy of sexual objectification and exploitation.

*Dealing With Sexual Harassment:*
*Writing A Letter to the Harasser*

One way of dealing with the sexual harasser is to write a confrontational letter. It is recommended that the letter itself be polite, low-key, and detailed. It should contain three parts: Part 1 detailing the facts without evaluation, Part 2 describing the victim's feelings, and Part 3 explaining what the victim wants next. The victim must also plan a way to deliver the letter for the best effect, and follow-up procedures.

From: Writing a letter to the sexual harasser: Another way of dealing with the problem, by the Association of American Colleges (1983), Washington DC. In: The Project on the Status and Education of Women, 12(3).

# Summary

Keeping women in their place:

| Crime | Condition* |
|-------|-----------|
| Incest | Lack of Trust |
| Rape | Fear |
| Battering | Isolation |
| Harassment | Inferiority |

*The four interacting factors are conditions present in all four victimizations—16 conditions.

The victims of incest, rape, battering and harassment all suffer from sexual objectification. That is the key to these four crimes of oppression. That objectification is prevalent in four personal conditions present in all four situations, but each condition may be especially characteristic of one specific victimization. Keep in mind that females who are early victims of incest are more likely to experience the other three forms of oppression. That means that the categories are interactive, progressive and dynamic.

As a victim of incest, a female child loses trust: trust in her father who uses her, trust in her mother who cannot protect her and trust in a world where her victimization goes unnoticed and where she has no control. She may learn to fight back with manipulation and deceit. Those may be the only weapons she has.

As a victim of rape, a female (often an adolescent) learns fear: fear of the dark, of strangers, of expressing her own sexuality, and fear of a violent death. As a result, girls must take on the lifestyles of prisoners in order to gain security. They may believe that they need protection, and to gain it they must become the property of a dominant man and be confined to the shelter of the family. Ironically, the protection females seek is often illusory and many victims are raped by their so-called protector. No doubt, experiencing rape reinforces the mistrust of females already exploited by their fathers.

As a victim of battering, a wife learns isolation: isolation from her family and friends who may blame her or do not want to get involved, from social agencies which may refuse to help her or may provide only token shelter, and from the culture which condones her victimization. As an abused wife, a woman may sink to the lowest kind of self image and the deepest form of alienation. She may become not only alienated from others, but, more significantly, she may grow to doubt herself out of feelings of powerlessness and dependency.

As a victim of harassment in the work place, a female employee learns to expect a position of inferiority: her jobs are delegated according to traditional ideas about the subservience of women, her ideas are discredited and she comes to view her value as decorative rather than substantive, and her boss has the right to use her services at whim, including her sexual services, as a condition of employment.

When women complain about their treatment, they may find that others do not want to hear about it, or blame them for the problem, or even condone the exploitation as "natural." That is true when females complain about incest, rape, battering or harassment. All four of these offenses are significant because they oppress all the women in our culture, even those who are not directly victimized. They create a climate of mistrust and fear between men and women. And by isolating females and reinforcing their inferiority, these four crimes make women second class citizens, a minority group cut off from access to power.  Because these acts reinforce the traditional structure of patriarchy, they serve to support the status quo and keep women in their subordinate place in it.

# *Note

There are countless articles, books, films, videos and pamphlets about the victimization of females now available. The subjects of rape and wife battering, in particular, have been covered extensively in many different types of approaches. It would be impossible to list every reference which is relevant to all the ideas presented in this chapter. To do so would mean a set of references after every sentence, and the text would be difficult to read as a result. Furthermore, it is really impossible to list even a small fraction of them here.

What follows is the most up-to-date list of publications having to do with the victimization of women that could be derived. With the exception of a few significant prior sources, all of the publications listed below came out after 1980. The bibliography has been organized the same way as Chapter 5. There are alphabetical lists of references corresponding to each of the topics covered in the text.

Chapter 5 would not have been possible without the research assistance of Theresa Donawell, Senta Parker and Raymond Kelly. The National Criminal Justice Reference Service also provided an extensive collection of references about the four types of victimization.

# References

### The Victimization of Women

Burgess, A. (1984).   Intra-familial sexual abuse. In J. Campbell & J. Humphreys (Eds.), *Nursing care of victims of family violence*. Reston, VA: Reston Publishing Co.

Bureau of Justice Statistics (1984).   *Criminal victimization in the United States*. Washington, D.C.: U.S. Department of Justice.

Chaneles, S. (1984).   *Gender issues, sex offenses, and criminal justice*.   New York: Haworth Press.

Edwards, S. (1983).   Sexual offenses and conceptions of victims in the criminal justice process. *Victimology*, 8(3-4), 113-130.

Goldstein, R. (1982).   New dimensions of expertise in psychiatry and criminal law. In R. Rosner (Ed.), *Critical issues in American psychiatry and the law*. Springfield, IL: Charles C. Thomas.

Hepperle, W.L. (1985).   Women victims in the criminal justice system. In I. Moyer (Ed.), *Changing roles of women in the criminal justice system*. Prospect Heights, IL: Waveland.

Hirsch, M.F.(1981).   *Women and violence*. New York: Van Nostrand-Reinhold.

Laub, J.H. (1981).   Ecological considerations in victim reporting to the police. *Journal of Criminal Justice*, 9(6), 419-430.

Klein, D. (1981).   Violence against women—Some considerations regarding its causes and its elimination. *Crime And Delinquency*. 27(1), 64-80.

Rafter, N. & Natalizia, E. (1981).   Marxist feminism—Implications for criminal justice. *Crime and Delinquency*, 27(1), 81-98.

Revitch, E. (1980).   Gynocide and unprovoked attacks on women. *Corrective and Social Psychiatry and Journal of Behavior Technology Methods and Therapy*, 26(1), 6-11.

Russell, D. (1984).   *Sexual exploitation*.   Beverly Hills: Sage Library of Social Research, 155.

Uniform Crime Reports (1986).   *Crime in the U.S., 1985*. Washington, D.C.: Federal Bureau of Investigation.

U.S. Department of Health and Human Services (1984).   *Sexual Exploitation*. Beverly Hills: Sage Library of Social Research, Vol. 155.

Wright, B. (1982).   Impact of changing sexual mores on the criminal justice system. In G. Stephens (Ed.), *The future of criminal justice*. Cincinnati, OH: Anderson.

## Incest

*Roles and Relationships—Father Dominant Patriarch*

Armstrong, L. (1978). Kiss daddy good-night. New York: Hawthorn Books.

Burgess, A., Groth, N. & McCausland, M. (1981). Child sex initiation rings. *American Journal of Orthopsychiatry.* 51(1), 110-119.

Butler, S. (1982). Politics of sexual assault. In S. Davidson (Ed.), *Justice for young women.* Tucson, AZ: New Directions for Young Women, Inc.

Courtois, C.A. (1982). Studying and counseling women with past incest experiences. *Victimology,* 5(2-4), 322-334.

DeYoung, M. (1983). Case reports—the sexual exploitation of incest victims by helping professionals. *Victimology,* 6(1-4), 92-101.

Felker, R. (1984). Incest—the need to develop a response to intra-family sexual abuse. *Duquesne Law Review,* 22(4), 901-925.

Finkelhor, D. (1980). *Long-term effects of childhood sexual victimization in a non-clinical sample.* Rockville, MD: NCJRS.

Finkelhor, D. (1982). Sexual abuse of boys. *Victimology,* 1(4), 76-84.

Finkelhor, D. (1984). *Child sexual abuse.* Riverside, NJ: Macmillan Publishing Co.

Gordon, L. & O'Keefe, P. (1985). Normality of incest. In A. Burgess (Ed.), *Rape and Sexual Assault.* New York: Garland.

Groff, M. & Hubble, L. (1984). Comparison of father-daughter and step-father-stepdaughter incest. *Criminal Justice and Behavior,* 11(4), 461-475.

Gruger, K. & Jones, R. (1983). Does sexual abuse lead to delinquent behavior? *Victimology,* 6(1-4), 85-91.

Linedecker, C. (1981). *Children in chains.* New York: Everest House.

Nasjleti, M. (1980). Suffering in silence—The male incest victim. *Child Welfare,* 59(5), 269-275.

Whitcomb, D. (1986). *When the victim is a child*. Washington, D.C.: U S Govt. Printing Office-NCJ 97664.


## The Cultural Signs — Sexual Objectification

Anson, R. (1980). Last porno show. In L. Schultz (Ed.), *Sexual victimology of youth*. Springfield, IL: Charles C. Thomas.

Goodwin, J. (1982). Cross-cultural perspectives on clinical problems of incest, *Sexual abuse*. Littleton, MA: John Wright.

Kempe, R. & Kempe, C. (1984). *Common secret*. San Francisco: W. H. Freeman & Co.

Rush, F. (1980). *The best kept secret*. Englewood Cliffs, NJ: Prentice-Hall.

Sgroi, S., Blick, L. & Porter, F. (1982). Conceptual framework for child sexual abuse. In S. Sgroi (Ed.), *Handbook of clinical intervention in child sexual abuse*. Lexington MA: D. C. Heath.

Tierney, K. & Corwin, D. (1983). Exploring intrafamilial child sexual abuse. In D. Finkelhor, et al (Ed.), *The dark side of families*. Beverly Hills: Sage.

Tilelli, J., Turek, D. & Jaffe, A. (1980). Sexual abuse of children. *New England Journal of Medicine*, 302(6), 319-323.


## The Law — Testimony of the Victims

Ahlgren, C. (1984). Maintaining incest victims' support relationships. *Journal of Family Law*, 22(3), 483-536.

Berliner, L. & Barbieri, M. (1984). Testimony of the child victim of sexual asault. *Journal of Social Issues*, 40(2), 125-137.

Schwartz, M. (1985). Incest victims and the criminal justice system. In I. Moyer (Ed.), *Changing roles of women in the criminal justice system*. Prospect Heights, IL: Waveland.

Tobias, J., Danto, B. & Robertson, R. (1980). The role of the police in dealing with sexually abused children. *Journal of Police Science and Administration*, 8(4), 464-473.

Weiss, E. & Berg, R. (1982). Child psychiatry and law—Child victims of sexual assault. *Journal of the American Academy of Child Psychiatry*, 21(5), 513-518.

### Incest Policy: Victim

Burgess, A. (1985). Sexual Victimization of Adolescents. In *Rape and sexual assault*. New York: Garland.

Sgroim, S. (1982). *Handbook of clinical intervention in child sexual abuse*. Lexington, MA: D. C. Heath.

Beck, J., Drakulich, P. & Gorham, C. (1980). Role of professionals in school or community settings. In C. Gorham (Ed.), *Rape and sexual assault*. Rockville, MD: Aspen Systems Corp.

### Incest Policy: Offender

Sagatun, I. (1982). Effects of court-ordered therapy on incest offenders. *Journal of Offender Counseling Services and Rehabilitation*, 5(3-4), 99-104.

### Incest Prevention: Situation

Sanford, L. (1980). *Silent children*. Garden City, New York: Anchor/Doubleday Press.

### Rape

### The Roles—Lover as Aggressor in Sexual Matters

Ageton, S. (1983). *Sexual assault among adolescents*. Lexington, MA: D. C. Heath.

Amir, M. (1971). *Patterns in forcible rape*. Chicago: University of Chicago Press.

Becker, J. et al (1982). The effects of sexual assault on rape and attempted rape victims. *Victimology*, 7(1-4), 106-113.

Brownmiller, S. (1975). *Against our will: Men, women and rape*. New York: Simon & Schuster.

Burgess, A. (1985). *Rape and sexual assault*. New York: Garland.

Burt, M. & Albin, R. (1981). Rape myths, rape definitions and probability of conviction. *Journal of Applied Social Psychology*, 11(3), 212-230.

Clark, L. & Lewis, D. (1977). *Rape — The price of coercive sexuality*. Toronto: Women's Education Press.

Dean, C. & deBruyn-Kops, M. (1982). *Crime and the consequences of rape*. Springfield, IL: Charles C. Thomas.

Deming, M. & Eppy, A. (1981). Sociology of rape. *Sociology and Social Research*, 65(4), 357-380.

Ellis, L. & Beattie, C. (1983). Feminist explanation for rape. *Journal of Sex Research*, 19(1), 74-93.

Fortune, M. (1983). *Sexual violence — The unmentionable sin*. New York: Pilgrim Press.

Gibbons, D. (1983). Forcible rape — Current knowledge and research issues. *Criminal Justice Abstracts*, March, 100-112.

Griffin, S. (1982). Rape: the all-American crime. In B. Raffel-Price & N. Sokoloff (Eds.), *The criminal justice system and women*. New York: Clark-Boardman.

Groth, A. et al (1977). Rape: power, anger and sexuality. *The American Journal of Psychiatry*, 134(1) 1239-1243.

Hageman, M. (1981). At-risk crime populations. *Journal of Police Science and Administration*, 9(2), 184-187.

Hall, E. & Flanner, P. (1984). Prevalence and correlates of sexual assault experiences in adolescents. *Victimology*, 9(3-4), 398-406.

Hindelang, M., Gottfredson, M. & Garofalo, J. (1980). Toward a Theory of Personal Criminal Victimization. In E. Bitner, & S. Messinger (Eds), *Criminology Review Yearbook*, VOL. 2. Beverly Hills: Sage.

Horos, C. (1981). *Rape*. New York: Dell.

Johnson, A. (1980). On the prevalence of rape in the U.S., *Signs*, 6(11), 136-146.

Kanin, E. & Parcell, S. (1981). Sexual aggression. In L. Bowker (Ed.), *Women and crime in America*. New York: Glencoe.

Kanin, E. (1984). Date rape. *Victimology*, 9(1), 95-108.

Lebeau, J. (1985). Some problems with measuring and describing rape presented by the serial offender. *Justice Quarterly*, 2(3), 385-398.

LeDoux, J. & Hazelwood, R. (1985). Police attitudes and beliefs toward rape. *Journal of Police Science and Administration*, 13(3), 211-220.

Randall, S. & Rose, V. (1981). Barriers to becoming a 'successful' rape victim. In L. Bowker (Ed.), *Women and crime in America*. Riverside, NJ: Macmillan.

Sanday, P. (1981). Socio-cultural context of rape—A cross-cultural study. *Journal of Social Issues*, 37(4), 5-27.

Scherer, J. (1982). Myth of passion. In J. Scherer and G. Shepherd (Eds.), *Victimization of the weak*. Springfield, IL: Charles C. Thomas.

Schwendinger, J. & Schwendinger, H. (1983). *Rape and inequality*. Beverly Hills: Sage.

Scully, D. & Marolla, J. (1985). Rape and vocabularies of motive. In A. Burgess (Ed.), *Rape and Sexual Assault*. New York: Garland Publishing, Inc.

Silbert, M. & Pines, A. (1981). Occupational hazards of street prostitutes. *Criminal Justice and Behavior*, 8(4), 395-424.

Smith, M. & Bennett, N. (1985). Poverty, inequality and theories of forcible rape. *Crime and Delinquency* (special issue), 31(2), 295-305.

Ruch, L. & Hennessy, M. (1982). Sexual assault: victim and attack dimensions. *Victimology*, 7(1-4), 94-105.

Russell, D. & Howell, N. (1983). Prevalence of rape in the U.S. revisited. *Signs*, 8(4), 688-695.

White, P. & Rollins, J. (1981). Rape—A family crisis. *Family Relations*, 30(1), 103-109.

Wood, P.L. (1981). Victim in a forcible rape case—A feminist view. In L. Bowker (Ed.), *Women and crime in America*. Riverside, NJ: Macmillan.

Zillman, D. (1984). *Connections between sex and aggression*. Hillsdale, NJ: Lawrence Erlbaum.

### Cultural Signs—Pornography

Abraham, S. et al. (1980). Pornography, obscenity and the law. New York: Facts on File, Inc.

Diamond, I. (1982). Pornography and repression—A reconsideration. In B. Raffel-Price & N. Sokoloff (Eds.), *The criminal justice system and women*. New York: Clark-Boardman.

Holmstrom, L. & Burges, A. (1983) Rape and everyday life. *Society*, 20(5), 33-40.

London, J. (1978). Image of violence against women. *Victimology*, 2(3-4), 510-524.

Malamuth, N. (1985). Mass media and aggression against women. In A. Burgess (Ed.), *Rape and sexual assault*. New York: Garland Publishing, Inc.

Parulski,Jr. G. (1980). Of skin and sin. *Police Product News*, 4(12), 34-39.

Patai, F. (1982). Pornography and woman battering. In M. Roy (Ed.), *Abusive Partner*. New York: Van Nostrand Reinhold.

Wheeler, H. (1985). Pornography and rape—A feminist perspective. In A. Burgess (Ed.), *Rape and sexual assault*. New York: Garland Publishing Co.


## The Law—Consent; Penetration

Borgida, E. & Brekke, N. (1985). Psycholegal research on rape trials. In A. Burgess (Ed.), *Rape and sexual assault*. New York: Garland Publishing, Inc.

Bristow, A. (1984). State v. Marks: An analysis of expert testimony on rape trauma syndrome. *Victimology*, 9(2), 273-281.

Charles, S. (1980). Sex crimes units are raising conviction rates, consciousness, costs...and questions. *Police Magazine*, 3(2), 52-61.

Clemmens, M. (1983). Elimination of the resistance requirement and other rape law reforms. *The Albany Law Review*, 47(3), 871-907.

Feild, H. (1979). Rape trials and jurors' decisions. *Law and Human Behavior*, 3(4), 261-284.

Feild, H. & Bienen, L. (1980). *Jurors and rape*. Lexington, MA: D. C. Heath.

Feldman-Summers, S. & Ashworth, C. (1981). Factors related to intentions to report a rape. *Journal of Social Issues*, 37(4), 53-70.

Fitzgerald, M. (1984). Sexual assault victim's prior sexual conduct admissible if three conditions met. *Marquette Law Review*, 67(2), 396-413.

Galvin, J. & Polk, K. (1983). Attrition in case processing. *Journal of Research in Crime and Delinquency*, 20(1), 126-154.

Hendricks, J. (1983). Criminal justice intervention with the rape victim. *Journal of Police Science and Administration*, 11(2), 225-232.

Hinch, R. (1985). Canada's new sexual assault laws. *Contemporary Crises*, 9(1), 33-44.

Holmstrom, L. & Burgess, A. (1983). *Victim of rape*. New Brunswick, NJ: Transaction Books.

LaFree, G. (1980). Variables affecting guilty pleas and convictions in rape processing. *Social Forces*, 58(3), 833-850.

LaFree, G. (1980). Effect of sexual stratification by race on official reactions to rape. *American Sociological Review*, 45(5), 842-854.

Lafree, G., Reskin, B. & Visher, C. (1985). Jurors' response to victim's behavior and legal issues in sexual assault trials. *Social Problems*, 32(4), 389-407.

Lasateer, M. (1980). Sexual assault—The legal framework. In C. Warner (Ed.), *Rape and sexual assault*. Rockville, MD: Aspen Systems Corporation.

LeBeau, J. (1984). Rape and racial patterns. *Journal of Offender Counseling, Services and Rehabilitation*, 9(1-2), 125-148.

Lizotte, A. (1985). Uniqueness of rape—Reporting assaultive violence to the police. *Crime and Delinquency* (special isssue), 31(2), 169-190.

Loh, W. (1981). What has reform of rape legislation wrought? *Journal of Social Issues*, 37(4), 28-52.

McGaughey, K. & Stiles, W. (1983). Courtroom interrogation of rape victims. *Journal of Applied Social Psychology*, 13(1), 78-87.

Marsh, J., Geist, A. & Caplan, N. (1982). *Rape and the limits of law reform*. Boston, MA: Auburn House Publishing Co.

Martin, P., et al (1985). Controversies surrounding the rape kit exam in the 1980's. *Crime and Delinquency* (special issue), 31(2), 223-246.

Nemeth, C. P. (1984). Legal emancipation for the victim of rape. *Human Rights*, 11(3), 30-35.

Nevling, F. (1982). Human body as a crime scene. *Law and Order*, 30(1), 40-44.

Osbourne, J. (1985). Rape law reform. In C. SchWeber & C. Feinman (Eds.), *Criminal justice politics and women*. New York: Haworth Press.

Polk, K. (1985). Rape reform and criminal justice processing. *Crime and Delinquency* (special issue), 31(2), 191-205.

Randall, S. & Rose, V. (1984).  Forcible rape. In R. Meier (Ed.), *The major forms of crime*. Beverly Hills: Sage.

Raum, B. (1983).  Rape trauma syndrome as circumstantial evidence of rape. *The Journal of Psychiatry and the Law*, 11(2), 203-213.

Schwartz, M. & Clear, T. (1980).  Toward a new law on rape. *Crime and Delinquency*, 26(2), 129-151.

Schwendinger, J. & Schwendinger, H. (1982).  Rape, the law, and private property. *Crime and Delinquency*, 28(2), 271-291.

Steger, M. (1985).  Impact of eligibility rules on female and male crime victims. *Justice System Journal*, 10(2), 193-212.

Sunday, S. & Tobach, E. (1985).  *A critique of the sociobiology of rape*. Staten Island, NY: Gordian Press, Inc.

Tanford, J. & Bocchino, A. (1980).  Rape victim shield laws and the sixth amendment. *University of Pennsylvania Law Review*, 128(3), 544-602.

Tchen, M. (1983).  Rape reform and a statutory consent defense. *Journal of Criminal Law and Criminology*, 74(4), 1518-1555.

U.S. Department of Justice Bureau of Justice Statistics, (1985).  *Crime of rape*. Rockville, MD: NIJ/NCJRS.

Williams, J. (1984).  Secondary victimization. *Victimology*, 9(1), 66-81.

Williams, K. (1981).  Few convictions in rape cases. *Journal of Criminal Justice*, 9(1), 29-39.

## Rape Policy: Victim

Alexander, C. (1980).  Blaming the victim. *Women and Health*,  5(1), 65-79.

Alexander, C. (1980).  Responsible victim. *Journal of Health and Social Behavior*, 21(1), 22-33.

Bart, P. (1981). Study of women who both were raped and avoided rape. *Journal of Social Issues*, 37(4), 123-137.

Burt, M. & Estep, R. (1983). Who is a victim? *Victimology*, 6(1-4), 15-28.

Booher, D. (1981). *Rape—What Would You Do If?* New York: Simon & Schuster.

Cohen, P. (1984). Resistance during sexual assaults—avoiding rape and injury. *Victimology*, 9(1), 120-129.

Ellis, E., Atkeson, B. & Calhoun, K. (1981). Assessment of long-term reaction to rape. *Journal of Abnormal Psychology*, 90(3), 263-266.

Fein, J. (1981). *Are you a target?* Belmont, CA: Wadsworth.

Feldman-Summers, S. & Norris, J. (1984). Differences between rape victims who report and those who do not report... *Journal of Applied Social Psychology*, 14(6), 562-573.

Fisher, W. (1980). Predicting injury to rape victims. In B. Price & P. Baunach (Eds.), *Criminal Justice Research*. Beverly Hills: Sage.

Fortune, M. (1984). *Sexual abuse prevention—For teenagers*. New York: United Church Press.

Gilmartin-Zena, P. (1983). Attribution theory and rape victim responsibility. *Deviant Behavior*, 4(3-4), 357-374.

Gilmartin-Zena, P. (1985). Rape impact. *Deviant Behavior*, 6(4), 347-361.

Gordon, M. et al. (1980). Crime, women and the quality of urban life. *Signs*, 5(3) supplement, 144-160.

Griffin, B. & Griffin, C. (1983). Victims in rape confrontation. *Victimology*, 6(1-4), 59-75.

Groth, A.N. & Burgess, A. (1980). Male rape—Offenders and victims. *American Journal of Psychiatry*, 137(7), 806-810.

Holmes, K. (1981). Services for victims of rape. *Social Casework*, 62(1), 30-39.

Kaufman, A. et al. (1980).   Male rape victims. *American Journal of Psychiatry*, 137(2), 221-223.

Kaufman, D., Rudeen, R. & Morgan, C. (1980).   *Safe within yourself—A woman's guide to rape prevention and self defense*. Alexandria, VA: Visage Press, Inc.

King, H. & Webb, C. (1981).   Rape crisis centers—Progress and problems. *Journal of Social Issues*, 37(4), 93-104.

London Rape Crisis Centre, (1984).   *Sexual Violence—The Reality For Women*. London: Women's Press Ltd.

Luginbuhl, J. & Mullin, C. (1981).   Rape and responsiblity. *Sex Roles*, 7(5), 547-559.

McCombie, S. (1980).   *Rape crisis intervention handbook*. New York: Plenum.

McGurn, T. & Kelly, C. (1984).   *Women's bible for survival in a violent society*. Victoria, Australia: Australian Association of Social Workers.

Mazelan, P. (1982).   Stereotypes and perceptions of the victims of rape. *Victimology*, 5(2-4), 121-132.

Morris, J. (1983).   *Victim Aftershock*. Danbury, CT: Franklin Watts.

Pugh, M. (1983).   Contributory fault and rape convictions—loglinear models for blaming the victim. *Social Psychology Quarterly*, 46(3), 233-242.

Ruch, L., Chandler, S. & Harter, R. (1980).   Life change and rape impact. *Journal of Health and Social Behavior*, 21(3), 248-260.

Sanders, W. (1980).   *Rape and woman's identity*. Beverly Hills: Sage.

Scacco Jr., A. (1982).   *Male Rape*  New York: AMS Press, Inc.

Schwartz, J., Williams, H. & Pepitone-Rockwell, F. (1983).   Constructon of a rape awareness scale. *Victimology*, 6(1-4), 110-119.

Schwendinger, J. & Schwendinger, H. (1980). Rape victims and the false sense of guilt. *Crime and Social Justice*, 13(1), 4-17.

Skelton, C. & Burkhart, B. (1980). Sexual assault—Determinants of victim disclosure. *Criminal Justice and Behavior*, 7(2), 229-236.

Smith, C., Marcus, P. & Brainerd, P. (1984). Defining a social problem and its solution. *Victimology*, 9(2), 234-246.

Smith, J. (1983). *Rape—Fight back and win!* South Hackensack, NJ: Stoeger Publishing Co.

Spaulding, D. (1980). Role of the victim advocate. In C. Warner (Ed.), *Rape and sexual assault*. Rockville, MD: Aspen Systems Corp.

Thornton, B. & Ryckman, R. (1983). Influence of a rape victim's physical attractiveness on attributions of responsibility. *Human Relations*, 36(6), 549-562.

Williams, J. & Holmes, K. (1981) The judgment of victims the social context of rape. *Journal of Sociology and Social Welfare*, 9(1), 154-169.

Williams, L. S. (1984). Classic rape—When do victims report? *Social Problems*, 31(4), 459-467.

Winkel, F. (1984). Changing misconceptions about rape...*Victimology*, 9(2), 262-272.

*Rape Policy: Offender*

Beneke, T. (1982). *Men on rape*. New York: St. Martins Press.

Bonheur, H. & Rosner, R. (1980). Sex Offenders, *Journal of Forensic Science*, 25(1), 3-14.

Hindelang, M. (1984). Variations in sex-race-age specific incidence rates of offending. In D. Georges-Abeyie (Ed.), *The criminal justice system and blacks*. New York: Clark Boardman Co.

Tirrell, F. & Aldridge, R. (1983).  Diagnostic classification of rape. *Corrective and Social Psychiatry and Journal of Behavior Technology Methods and Therapy*, 29(2), 56-62.

Malamuth, N. (1981).  Rape proclivity among males. *Journal of Social Issues*, 37(4), 138-157.

*Rape Policy: Situation*

Hauserman, N. & Lansing, P. (1981).  Rape on campus—postsecondary institutions as third party defendants. *Journal of College and University Law*, 8(2), 182-202.

McEvoy, A. & Brookings, J. (1984).  *If she is raped—A book for husbands, fathers and male friends*. Holmes Beach, FL: Learning Publications, Inc.

Muth, A. (1984).  Landlord liability. *Trial*, 20(3), 72-74, 76.

Phillips, D.M. (1986).  *Social policy and the legal response to rape—Annotated bibliography*. Monticello, IL: Vance Bibliographies.

Reynolds, L. (1984).  Rape: a social perspective. *Journal of Offender Counseling, Services and Rehabilitation*, 9(1-2), 149-160.

## Battering

*The Roles—Spouse Achieving Power Over His Property*

Bassett, S. (1980).  *Battered rich*. Port Washington, NY: Ashley Books, Inc.

Berk, R, et al (1983).  *Mutual combat and other family violence myths*. Beverly Hills: Sage.

Campbell, J. (1984).  Abuse of female partners. In J. Campbell, and J. Humphreys (Eds.), *Nursing care of victims of family violence*. Reston, VA: Reston Publishing Co.

Dobash, E. & Dobash, R. (1979).  *Violence against wives—A case against patriarchy*. New York: The Free Press.

Erchak, G. (1984). Escalation and maintenance of spouse abuse. *Victimology*, 9(2), 247-253.

Finkelhor, D. & Yllo, K. (1982). Forced sex in marriage. *Crime and Delinquency*, 28(3), 459-478.

Gentemann, K. (1984). Wife beating—attitudes of a non-clinical population. *Victimlogy*, 9(1), 109-119.

Kantor, S., Moore, K. & Opel, R. (1981). Family Violence in America—Symposium. *Vermont Law Review*, 6(2) & 7(1), 1-413.

Lincoln, A. & Strauss, M. (1985). *Crime and the family*. Springfild, IL: Charles C. Thomas.

Mills, T. (1984). Victimization and self-esteem—on equating husband abuse and wife abuse. *Victimology*, 9(2), 254-261.

National Clearinghouse on Domestic Violence (1980). *Battered Women—A National Concern*. Rockville, MD: NIJ/NCJRS.

Pagelow, M. (1981). *Women-battering*. Beverly Hills: Sage.

Pahl, J. (1985). *Private violence and public policy*. Boston: Routledge & Kegan Paul, Ltd.

Russell, D. (1982). *Rape in marriage*. Riverside, NJ: Macmillan Publishing Co., Inc.

Stacey, W. & Shupe, A. (1983). *The Family Secret*. Boston: Beacon Press.

Strauss, M. & Hotaling, G. (1980). *Social causes of husband-wife violence*. Minneapolis: University of Minnesota Press.

## The Cultural Sign—Value on Violence

Attorney General's Task Force, (1984). *Family violence*. Washington, D.C: U.S. Department of Justice.

Carbonel, D. et al (1984).  Violence against women. In Boston Women's Health Book Collective, *The new our bodies, ourselves.* New York: Simon and Schuster.

Feinman, C. (1987).  Domestic violence on the Navajo Nation Reservation. *Victimology,* forthcoming.

Finkelhor, D. et al (1983).  *Dark side of families.* Beverly Hills: Sage.

Hofeller, K. (1983).  *Battered women, shattered lives.* Palo Alto, CA: R & E Research.

Klein, D. (1982).  The dark side of marriage. In N. Rafter & E. Stanko (Eds.), *Judge, lawyer, victim, thief.* Ithaca, NY: Northeastern University Press.

Masumura, W. (1979).   Wife abuse and other forms of aggression. *Victimology,* 4(1), 46-59.

Martin, D. (1976). *Battered wives.* San Francisco: Glide Publications.

Rosenbaum, A. & O'Leary, K. (1981).  Marital violence—characteristics of abusive couples. *Journal of Counseling and Clinical Psychology,* 49(1), 63-71.

Stacey, W. & Shupe, A. (1983).  *Domestic violence in America.* Boston: Beacon Press.

Star, B. (1980).  Patterns in family violence. *Social Casework,* 61(6), 339-346.

Steinmetz, S. (1977).  The battered husband syndrome. *Victimology,* 2(3), 499-509.

Stockholm, K. & Helms, A. (1986).  *Domestic violence in Alaska—A preliminary report.* Orlando, FL: Annual meeting of the Academy of Criminal Justice Sciences.

Walker, L. (1985).   Battered women, psychology, and public policy. *American Psychologist,* 39(10), 1178-1182.

## The Law—Criminal and Civil Procedures

Bae, R. (1981). *Ineffective crisis intervention techniques—The case of the police*. New York: Pocket Books.

Barry, S. (1980). Spousal rape—The uncommon law. *American Bar Association Journal*, 66(1), 1088-1091.

Bell, D. (1985). Domestic violence—Victimization, police intervention, and disposition. *Journal of Criminal Justice*, 13(6), 525-534.

Berk, R. & Newton, P. (1985). Does arrest really deter wife battery? *American Sociological Review*, 50(2), 253-262.

Bochnak, E. (Ed.), (1981). *Women's self-defense cases—Theory and practice*. Charlottesville, VA: Michie Company.

Bolton Jr., F. (1980). Domestic violence continuum—A pressing need for legal intervention. *Women Lawyers Journal*, 66(1), 11-17.

Bowker, L. (1984). Battered wives and the police. *Police Studies*, 7(2), 84-93.

Boylan, A., et al (1982). *Legal advocacy for battered women*. Washington, DC: National Center on Women and Family Law.

Brown, L. (1980). Admissibility of expert testimony on the subject of battered women. *Criminal Justice Journal*, (491), 161-179.

Brown, S. (1984). Police responses to wife beating—Neglect of a crime of violence. *Journal of Criminal Justice*, 12(3), 277-288.

Catrell, L. (1984). On trial. *The National Law Journal*, 30(1), 6.

Costa, J. (1983). *Abuse of women—Legislation, reporting and prevention*. Lexington, MA: D.C. Heath & Co.

Eber, L. (1981). Battered wife's dilemma—To kill or to be killed. *Hastings Law Journal*, 32(4), 895-931.

Eisenberg, A. & Seymour, E. (1980). Defending battered women. *Trial*, 16(12), 30-33, 61.

Elli, R. (1980). Legal wrongs of battered women. In Z. Bankowski & G. Mungham (Eds.), *Essays in law and society*. Boston: Routledge and Kegan Paul, Ltd.

Freeman, M. (1981). But if you can't rape your wife, who(m) can you rape? *Family Law Quarterly*, 15(1), 1-29.

Glasgow, J.M. (1980). Marital rape exemption—Legal sanction of spouse abuse. *Journal of Family Law*, 18(1), 565-586.

Grau, J., etc. (l985). Restraining orders for battered women. In C. SchWeber & C. Feinman (Eds.), *Criminal justice politics and women*. New York: Haworth Press.

Harmen, J. (1984). Consent, harm and marital rape. *Journal of Family Law*, 22(3), 423-443.

Homant, R. & Kennedy, B. (1985). Police perception of spouse abuse: a comparison of male and female officers. *Journal of Criminal Justice*, 13(1), 29-47.

Jeffords, C. & Dull, R. (1982). Demographic variations in attitudes toward marital rape immunity. Journal of *Marriage and the Family*, August, 755-762.

Klatt, M. R. (1980). Rape in marriage. *Baylor Law Review*, 32(1), 109-121.

Kuhl, A. & Saltzman, L. (1985). Battered women and the criminal justice system. In Moyer, I. (Ed.), *The changing roles of women in the criminal justice system*. Prospect Heights, IL: Waveland Press.

Lerman, L. G. (1980). *Legal help for battered women*. Rockville, MD.: National Clearinghouse on Domestic Violence, NIJ/NCJRS.

Loseke, D. & Cahill, S. (1984). Social construction of deviance—experts on battered women. *Social Problems*, 31(3), 296-310.

Larman, L. (1982). *Legal help for battered women*. Washington, D.C.: Center for Women Policy Study.

Loving, N. (1980). *Responding to spouse abuse and wife beating—A guide for police*. Washington, DC: Police Executive Research Forum.

Munson, P. (1980). Protecting battered wives—The availability of legal remedies. *Journal of Sociology and Social Welfare*, 7(4), 586-600.

Pagelow, M. (1981). Secondary battering and alteratives of female victims of spouse abuse. In L. Bowker (Ed.), *Women and crime in America*. Riverside, NJ: Macmillan Publishing Co., Inc.

Reamey, G. (1983). Legal remedial alternatives for spouse abuse in Texas. *Houston Law Review*, 20(5), 1279-1320.

Walter, P. (1982). Expert testimony and battered women. *Journal of Legal Medicine*, 3(2), 267-294.

### Battering Policy: Victims

Bowker, L. & Maurer, L. (1985). Importance of sheltering in the lives of battered women. *Response*, 8(1), 2-8.

Constantino, C. (1981). Intervention with battered women. *Social Work*, 26(6), 456-460.

Epstein, W. (1984). Get thee to a shelter. *Journal of Sociology and Social Welfare*, 11(2), 366-380.

Ferraro, K. (1983). Rationalizing violence—How battered women stay. *Victimology*, 8(3-4), 203-212.

Fiedler, D., Briar, K. & Pierce, M. (1984). Services for battered women. *Journal of Sociology and Social Welfare*, 1193), 540-557.

Galaway, B. & Hudson, J. (1981). *Perspectives on crime victims*, St. Louis: C.V. Mosby Co.

Green, H. (1984). *Turning fear to hope*. Nashville, TN: Thomas Nelson, Inc.

Kiebert, I. & Schechter, S. (1980). *Park Slope Safe Homes Project*, Brooklyn. Albany: NY State Department of Social Services.

Miller, D. (1982). Innovative program development for battered women and their families. *Victimology*, 5(2-4), 335-346.

Neidig, P. (1984). Women's shelters, men's collectives and other issues in the field of spouse abuse. *Victimology*, 9(3), 464-476.

NiCarthy, G. (1982). *Getting free—A handbook for women in abusive relationships.* Seattle: Seal Press.

Roberts, A. & Roberts, B. (1981). *Sheltering battered women.* New York: Springer Publishing Co.

Roundtree, G., et al (1982). Survey of the types of crimes committed by incarcerated females in two states who reported being battered. *Corrective and Social Psychiatry and Journal of Behavior Technology Methods and Therapy*, 28(1), 23-26.

Walker, L. (1978). Battered women and learned helplessness, *Victimology*, 2(3-4), 525-534.

*Battering Policy: Offenders*

Bowker, L (1983). *Beating wife-beating.* Lexington, MA: D.C. Heath.

Brown, M., Aquirre, B. & Jorgensen, C. (1981). Abusers of clients of women's shelters. *Journal of Sociology and Social Welfare*, 8(3), 462-470.

Coates, C. & Leong, D. (1980). Conflict and communication for women and men in battering relationships. *Denver anti-crime council.* Rockville, MD:NIJ/NCJRS.

Deschner, J. (1984). *The hitting habit: Anger control for battering couples.* New York: The Free Press.

Myers, T. & Gilbert, S. (1983). Wifebeaters' group through a women's center. *Victimology*, 8(1-2), 238-248.

Neidig, P. (1985). *Domestic conflict containment.* Beaufort, SC: Behavioral Science Associates, Inc.

Roy, M. (1982). *Abusive partner.* New York: Van Nostrand Reinhold.

Sarkin, D. et al (1985). *The male batterer.* New York: Springer Publishing Co., Inc.

Sherman, L. & Berk, R. (1984). The specific deterrent effects of arrest for domestic assault. *American Sociological Review*, 49(2), 261-272.

Shields, N. & Hanneke, C. (1983). Attribution processes in violent relationships. *Journal of Applied Social Psychology*, 13(6), 515-527.

Sonking, D. & Durphy, M. (1982). *Learning to live without violence.* San Francisco: Volcano Press.

VanHasselt, V. et al (1985). Alcohol use in wife abusers and their spouses. *Addictive Behaviors*, 10(2), 127-135.


### Battering Policy: Situation

Barnes, S. (1985). Psychosocial aspects of wife abuse in the U.S. *Journal of Crisis Intervention*, 2(2), 29-36.

Giles-Sims, J. (1983). *Wife battering: A systems theory approach.* New York: The Guilford Press.

Loeb, R. (1983). Program of community education for dealing with spouse abuse. *Journal of Community Psychology*, 11(1), 241-252.

Long, K. (1986). Cultural considerations in the assessment and treatment of intrafamilial abuse. *American Journal of Orthopsychiatry*, 48(1), 131-136.

Yoder, D. (1982). Spouse assault—a community approach. In S. Cronk (Ed.), *Criminal Justice in Rural America.* Rockville, MD: NIJ/NCJRS.


### Dealing With the Problem—The Military Family

McNelis, P. (1985). Military Family Programs. *Psychotherapy in Private Practice*, 3(2), 79-86.

West, L., et al (1981). *Wife abuse in the armed forces.* Washington, D.C.: Center for Women Policy Studies.

## Sexual Harassment in the Workplace

*The Role—Boss Taking the Privileges to Which He Is Due*

Collins, E. & Blodgett, T. (1981). Sexual harassment...some see it...some won't. *Harvard Business Review*, 59(20), 76.

Korda, M. (1972). *Male chauvinism: How it works*. New York: Random House.

MacKinnon, C. (1979). *Sexual harassment of working women*. Yale: Yale University Press.

McCaghy, M. (1985). *Sexual harassment: A guide to resources*. Boston: G. K. Hall, & Co.

National Survey on Sexual Harassment (1981). *Harvard Business Review*. Boston: Harvard Business Review Reprint Service.

Schneider, B. (1982). Consciousness about sexual harassment among heterosexual and lesbian women workers. *Journal of Social Issues*, 38(4), 75-98.

U.S. Merit Systems Protection Board (1981). *Sexual Harassment in the Federal Workplace*. Washington D.C.: U.S. Government Printing Office.

University of Wisconsin Affirmative Action Office (1982). *An Annotated Guide to Materials on Sexual Harassment*. Madison, WS: Affirmative Action Center(1980).

Abusing sex at the office. *Newsweek*, March 10, 81-82.

*The Cultural Sign—The Economic Position of Women*

Blackhouse, C. (1981). *Sexual harassment on the job*. University of Wisconsin, Madison: Business Library.

Brewer, M. & Berk, R. (1982). Beyond nine to five. *Journal of Social Issues*, 38(1), 149-158.

Brewer, M. (1982). Further beyond nine to five. *Journal of Social Issues*, 38(4) 1-4.

Farley, L. (1978). *Sexual Shakedown*. New York: McGraw-Hill.

### The Law—Losses and Gains

Barnes, W. (1981). Let me call you quota, sweetheart. *Commentary*, 71(6), 48.

Guidelines on Discrimination Because of Sex, Title VII (1980). Sexual Harassment. *Federal Register*, 45(219), 74676-77.

Howard, S (1983). Title VII sexual harassment guidelines and educational employment. *Project on the Status and Education of Women*. Washington, D.C.: The Association of American Colleges, 12(3).
(1980).

*Legal Remedies for Sexual Harassment*. Washington, D.C: Women's Legal Defense Fund.

Livingston, J. (1982). Responses to sexual harassment on the job: legal, organizational, and individual actions. *Journal of Social Issues*, 4(5) 5-22.

Marmo, M. (1980). Arbitrating sexual harassment cases. *Arbitration Journal*, 35(1), 35-40.

Tangri, S. et al (1982). Sexual harassment at work: three explanatory models. *Journal of Social Issues*, 38(4) 33-54.

### Sexual Harassment Policy: Victim

Alliance Against Sexual Coercion (1981). *Strategies for change—Working women and sexual harassment*. Cambridge, MA: Alliance Against Sexual Coercion.

Jensen, I. & Gutek, B. (1982). Attributions and assignment of responsibility in sexual harassment. *Journal of Social Issues*, 38(4), 121-136.

Bettner, J. (1979).  How to tame the office wolf without getting bitten. *Business Week*, 1, 107-108.

Curtis, J. (1980).  Sexual Harassment: What it is; how to deal with it successfully. *Business and Professional Women*, 36(6), 4-6.


### Sexual Harassment Policy:  Offender

Lublin, J. (1981).  Resisting advances: employers act to curb sex harassing on the job. *Wall Street Journal*, 104(24), 1.

Zemke, R. (1981).  Sexual harassment: Is training the key? *Training*, February.


### Sexual Harassment Policy:  Situation

Gordon, F. & Strober, J. (Eds.), (1980).  *Bringing women into management*. New York: McGraw-Hill.

Neugarten, D. & Shafritz, J. (1980).  *Sexuality in organizations*. Oak Park, IL: Moore Publishing Co.

Rowe, M. (1981).  Dealing with sexual harassment. *Harvard Business Review*, 59(4), 42.

Schmidt, P. (1981).  How to handle sexual harassment on campus. *Glamour*, 79(3), 329.

Vermont Advisory Committee to the U.S. Commission on Civil Rights (1982). *Sexual harassment on the job: A guide for employers*. Mt. Pelier, VT: State Personnel Office.

# 6

# Criminal Justice Occupations for Women

## Introduction

It is only since the 1970s that significant numbers of women have come to occupy positions in the criminal justice profession. Several case illustrations will show that women who enter these occupations not only reap the benefits but also face the associated problems. Further, as women in traditionally male occupations, they stand out and are probably more subject to public scrutiny for their actions. For example:

ROSE ELIZABETH BIRD. In 1977 she was the first woman appointed Chief Justice of the California State Supreme Court. In 1965 she was the first female clerk for a judge on the Nevada Supreme Court; in 1966 she was the first woman hired by the Santa Clara County public defenders office, and she was the first female cabinet officer appointed by a California governor. Her opposition to the death penalty made her the target of conservative groups who saw her as too soft on crime, and in 1986 she became the first Chief Justice in California's history to be unseated by the voters (Epstein, 1981; Jenkins, 1985; Culver and Wold, 1986, Lindsey, 1986).

PENNY E. HARRINGTON. In January of 1985 she became the first woman police chief in a large U.S. city when she was selected as chief for Portland, Oregon. She had worked her way up the ranks since 1964 and was active in a series of sex discrimination suits against the department. Within one month of taking office, budget cuts required her to lay off 16 officers and leave 60 vacancies open in the 760-member force. She was at odds with patrol officers over a hold they used which resulted in the death of one suspect, and her husband, who was an officer on the force, was accused of leaking information of a pending drug bust. She offered her resignation in June of 1986 after an investigating commission suggested that she step down as a result of her handling of department problems. In October of 1986 she won a disability claim based on the stress resulting from the controversy and her subsequent retirement (O'Neill, 1986:12; "Portland's tarnished Penny," 1986:26; "Ex-chief of police," 1986).

DONNA PAYANT. On May 15, 1981, less than a month after she graduated from the training academy, Donna Payant became the first female correctional officer in the United States killed in the line of duty. She was killed while working at the Green Haven State Correctional Facility in New York by a man already sentenced to three 25-year-to-life terms who strangled her and placed her body in a dumpster, where it was found the next day at a landfill 25 miles away. Her husband was a correctional officer at another institution (McFadden, 1981:37; Saxon, 1981:31).

This chapter will examine the role of women as criminal justice professionals in a variety of tasks. Until recently, women have played relatively minor roles as criminal justice professionals. During World War II, when a number of young men were in the military, women found more opportunities in such areas as law and policing. However, when the war ended the pre-war patterns of sex-based hiring returned and opportunities for women were again restricted.

There is no doubt that part of the trend toward hiring women in previously all-male criminal justice occupations can be attributed to changing views about appropriate roles for women. It would be a mistake, however, to make too much of changing public sentiments. In male-dominated professions those doing the hiring are primarily males whose training and social experiences have reinforced the idea that some jobs are simply not appropriate for women, particularly jobs which require working with adult male criminal offenders. Further, institutions in general are known for their resistance to change. Several authors have suggested that the growing numbers of women in criminal justice professions is attributed largely to court and legislative mandates which have *forced* changes in hiring policies. Across a variety of criminal justice occupations the pattern has been the same. Strong resistance to the hiring of women is followed by a gradual acceptance of them *after* they have been hired and have proven themselves—a process which will often require more than one generation of females. Further, the pressures are always the greatest on those women who are the groundbreakers, for they often must overachieve for their efforts to be recognized.

Much of the discussion that follows focuses on how women have "broken into" the criminal justice profession, but we will also see that they are a long way from full acceptance. While overt discrimination is seldom tolerated, more subtle forms still persist. We will also see that although this general pattern applies, each criminal justice profession presents unique problems and issues in the hiring of females.

## The Legal Profession

The U.S. Bureau of Labor Statistics estimates that about 16 percent of the nation's lawyers and judges in 1984 were women (U.S. Bureau of the Census, 1985:402). This may seem a small figure, particularly when one considers that women now make up half of all students in many law schools (Fossum, 1983). However, the difference between the proportion of women in the legal profession and their representation among law school students dramatically illustrates just how rapidly women are entering the profession. As Barbara Curran's data has shown, "women lawyers were less than 3 percent of the lawyer population during the entire period from 1951 through 1970 but 8.1 percent in 1980 and almost 13 percent in 1984 (1986:25)." Ironically, the number of women entering the field of law has grown at precisely the same time that there may be too many lawyers. Curran (1986), for example, reports that in 1951 there were 221,605 lawyers in the U.S., but by 1984 this figure had increased to 649,000. Law school graduates, including women, are finding it more and more difficult to secure employment upon graduation (Fossum, 1983).

The large number of women now entering the legal profession represents the result of a long and slow process. In 1869, Iowa became the first state to admit a woman to the bar when it admitted Arabella A. Mansfield. Other states, however, were slow to follow Iowa's example:

Scarcely two months after Arabella Mansfield was admitted to the Iowa bar, Myra Bradwell passed an examination for the Chicago bar, but the Illinois Supreme Court refused to grant her a license to practice law on the grounds of her sex....In other landmark cases Lavinia Goodell was refused admission to the Wisconsin bar in 1875, Lelia Josephine Robinson was refused

admission to the bar of Massachusetts in 1881, and Belva
Lockwood, although admitted to the District of Columbia bar
and admitted to practice before the United States Supreme
Court, was still refused admission to the Virginia bar in the
1890s because of her sex (Weisberg, 1977:485-86).

Other obstacles discouraged women from entering the law. For many
years, women were barred from prestigious law schools—Harvard did not
admit women until 1950 and Notre Dame did not admit women until 1969
(Weisberg, 1977:486). Where women were admitted to law schools, they
often faced hostile instructors, and in some cases prospective employers
refused to interview them on campus (Epstein, 1981:187). Women who did
manage to get law degrees found they were then barred from membership
in professional associations. For example, "The Woman Lawyer's Club
(which became the National Association of Women Lawyers in 1911) was
founded in 1899 because the American Bar Association did not admit
women (Epstein, 1981:259)." Further, it was not until the 1970s and 1980s
that women were allowed to participate at decision-making levels in bar
associations (Epstein, 1981:254).

Given the hostile or exclusive environment of the most prestigious law
schools, many women chose to attend part-time law schools which were less
"discriminating" in their admission practices. One school, the Portia Law
School, was established in 1908 as the first and only law school exclusively
for women. At its peak in 1929, Portia was enrolling about 30 percent of all
women in law schools in the United States (Chester, 1985). While the
quality of instruction at these part-time institutions was high, the most
prestigious law firms preferred to recruit from more "established" law
schools. In reality, however, large law firms were reluctant to hire females
regardless of their educational background, often justifying their decisions
on the grounds that clients would feel uncomfortable with their affairs being
handled by a woman, women could not attend business lunches which were
often held at "men-only" clubs, and some law firms even cited the lack of
bathroom facilities—not intending to allow a female associate to use the
same bathroom as lowly secretaries.

Although the number of female attorneys began to gradually increase
from the turn of the century forward, the general pattern of resistance to
women in the law continues until the present. Further, it is only since the
1970s that women have played active and visible roles in the legal
profession. Prior to the 1970s many women lawyers were restricted to
serving as legal secretaries, or to performing low status assignments in areas
such as probate, family law, and juvenile law. Sandra Day O'Connor, named
the first female Associate Justice of the Supreme Court in 1981, found that

even though she graduated third in her class from the Stanford law school in 1953 (William Rehnquist, now Chief Justice of the Supreme Court, was first), her first job offer was as a legal secretary (Bodine, 1983).

It is ironic that the law itself has been used to dismantle roadblocks to women seeking a career in law. Legislative changes and a series of successful court cases in the 1970s and early 1980s have significantly changed the prospects for women entering law. For example:

> In the late 1960s and early 1970s a series of ten lawsuits were brought against some of the nation's most prestigious law firms charging them with sex discrimination in hiring and promotion. These suits were settled with the firms agreeing to increase the number of women in their firms (Abramson and Franklin, 1986:22).

> 1971—Women students filed and won a lawsuit against the State Board of Examiners of New York for discriminating against women in bar examination procedures, including the segregation of women during the exam (Epstein, 1981:72).

> 1972—A series of amendments to Title VII were passed that extended its provision to all employers with fifteen or more workers and gave the EEOC the power to initiate suits. Of particular relevance for lawyers, legislation defined law school placement offices as employment offices and thus made them targets for suits (Epstein, 1981:94).

> 1984—The U.S. Supreme Court held in Hinshon v. King and Spaulding that law firms could not discriminate against women in decisions to promote associates to full partners. Elizabeth Hinshon was only the second woman hired by a 102-lawyer Atlanta firm, which had never admitted a woman to partnership in its 100-year history. The case made national news because one of the firm's senior partners was former U.S. Attorney General Griffin Bell (McNamara, 1986:430).

These legal actions, and others, have forced law schools and employers to examine their policies regarding the education, hiring, and promotion of women. As a result, there are major changes, not only in the number of women entering law, but in the kinds of specialties to which these women are drawn. Women are increasingly drawn to the same kinds of specialties that attract men to the profession, and women no longer feel strong social pressures to limit themselves to such low-status areas as matrimonial, poverty, or public interest law. Further, large firms are increasingly willing to hire and promote female associates (Curran, 1986:45), and within these large firms women are less likely than ever to find themselves channeled into "women's areas," such as estates or trusts.

Given the rapid rate at which women have entered the legal profession, the full extent to which their presence will impact the profession is still unknown. Several studies, however, suggest likely trends. The first was a national telephone survey of 605 lawyers conducted for the American Bar Association in 1983 and reported in the *American Bar Association Journal* (Winter, 1983). The study found that males were overwhelmingly accepting of women lawyers, and felt they would have little overall impact on the discipline. The most frequently cited reason given by women for entering law was the adversarial nature of the work and most of the women were satisfied with the occupation. The women in the survey were more likely than the men to have finished in the top 10 percent of their classes, but members of both sexes felt that women faced a tougher job market than men. Male lawyers thought that women were generally harder working and more conscientious, but faulted them for being over-emotional and abrasive in their professional roles. Although law firms followed no universal rules concerning maternity leave, 87 percent of the women lawyers who took a leave of absence to have a baby returned to work within six months, and there was overwhelming agreement that it was realistic to combine the role of lawyer with that of wife and mother. A relatively small percent (17 percent of the women and 7 percent of the men) believed that men and women lawyers were treated differently, and these differences generally resulted in women being given less responsibility and fewer choice assignments—which would ultimately hinder their chances for promotion. It is also worth noting that although male respondents were relatively egalitarian in this 1983 study, fully 65 percent of the males worked in firms with no female colleagues. Overall, the results of this national survey suggest a relatively smooth transition and general acceptance of women into the legal profession.

In contrast to the optimistic picture painted by the 1983 ABA study, a 1986 study by the New York Task Force on Women in the Courts documents a myriad of ways in which female attorneys still face discrimination. The study, based on testimony before the commission and a survey of 1,759 attorneys in the state of New York, focused on females as attorneys, offenders, and victims in the courts. In this study, male and female attorneys had very different perceptions about the treatment of female attorneys in the courts. For example, the majority of women (82 percent) compared with only 45 percent of the men reported instances in which judges addressed women attorneys by first names or terms of endearment when men were addressed by surnames or titles. Similarly, over two-thirds of the women but only about one-fourth of the men reported sexist comments by judges as happening often or sometimes. Further, few attorneys of either sex reported instances in which judges intervened to correct sexist remarks by opposing counsel. The manner in which judges and opposing male attorneys blatantly mistreat female attorneys is well illustrated by examples provided in the commission report:

> THIRTY-FIVE YEAR OLD FEMALE: I have personally been invited to sit on the lap of a landlord/tenant judge while arguing a motion before the judge (p. 220).

> TWENTY-NINE YEAR OLD FEMALE: Judge repeatedly refers to female attorneys as "dear" or "young lady" while males are referred to as "Mr." This is done in open court and obviously affects witness response as well as client confidence. I've heard male attorneys make such overtly sexist comments as, "Fix your slip, you're giving me a hard-on" and "You pain in the ass women should be home where you belong—in bed." This was said in open court, again with no chastisement by the court...(p. 212).

> A NASSAU COUNTY SUPREME COURT JUSTICE was admonished after he, over a period of years, referred to female attorneys as "kitten," "bitch" and "Jewish-American Princess," commented on physical attributes such as a "well-endowed chest" and "great legs," and remarked that attractive women attorneys could have anything they asked for (p. 213).

> A BROOKLYN SUPREME COURT JUSTICE was publicly censured for calling a woman attorney "little girl." The judge defended his remarks by saying that calling a woman attorney "little girl" was no different from calling her "sweetheart" or "darling," implying that such comments are not inappropriate (p. 213).

Taken together, the New York and ABA studies suggest that, although they are playing an increasingly active role in the legal profession, women are by no means fully accepted. It is unclear why the two studies yielded such very different results, but several explanations are possible. First, the ABA study focused only on attorneys and on women as colleagues. The improper behavior of attorneys noted in the New York study was largely from opposing counsel—who may have used them in a tasteless ploy to gain a psychological edge in the court proceedings. Secondly, the New York study focused greater attention on the actions of judges. Since younger male attorneys appear more accepting of women as attorneys than do more experienced males, the actions of these judges may be more understandable (though certainly not justifiable) in that judges are usually drawn from attorneys with extensive experience. Many of these judges, for example, probably had few or no females in their law school classes. Such judges may represent a dying breed who are no longer characteristic of the larger legal profession but whose discriminatory attitude is nevertheless damaging.

## Women as Law School Faculty

Not only will women entering law school find themselves in the company of other female students, but there are more female law professors than there were just 20 years ago. For female law students, women law professors provide important role models and may serve as mentors or sponsors whose personal contacts facilitate job seeking. In addition, the extent to which women occupy such high status positions as law professors is one measure of their acceptance by the profession.

The number of female law faculty members has increased dramatically in recent years, from 1.7 percent in 1967 to 19.5 percent by 1985 (Fossum, cited in Faught, 1986:453). As in other areas of law, at least part of this trend is attributable to a fear of legal actions charging discrimination. In the past, however, there were also structural barriers to prevent women from teaching in law schools. For example, the typical path to academic law involves at least four steps: (1) outstanding legal credentials, (2) service as an editor of a law review, (3) clerking for a judge of outstanding reputation, preferably a Supreme Court judge or Federal Court of Appeals judge, and (4) support through an informal referral system by which law school professors recommend (former) outstanding students to other law schools looking for professors. While women have an outstanding track record of academic performance in law school, in the past they have been at a decided disadvantage in terms of the other three criteria (Weisberg, 1979). Until recently their chances of serving as editor of a major law review were slim and many judges openly refused to take on female clerks. It was not until the 1970s, for example, that women had much hope of clerking for Supreme Court Justices (Epstein, 1981). Further, until relatively recently, nepotism laws prevented husbands and wives from serving on the same faculty, a particular problem for couples who met in law school and pursued parallel careers.

When women were hired they often found themselves in stereotypically female roles—as law librarians or as specialists in family law (Epstein, 1981; Faught, 1986; Weisberg, 1979). Further, in her 1976-78 survey of law school programs, Weisberg (1979) found that women were not evenly distributed across law schools. The most prestigious law schools tended to have fewer than average women and many schools had no women at all.

While there has been a large increase in the number of women law professors between 1967 and 1985, Faught (1986) has argued that the reduced demand for legal education will slow the influx of female law faculty. There will simply be fewer new faculty of either sex hired as departments reduce the size of their faculty by not replacing those who retire. Epstein (1981) also argues that further dramatic increases in the number of female law faculty are unlikely in the near future.

## Women as Judges

All of the factors which have traditionally kept women from becoming lawyers and law school professors have also restricted their access to the judiciary. The rise of women in the judiciary was an extremely slow process. By 1900 a majority of the states had admitted at least one woman to the bar, but only 3 women had served in any judicial capacity, and these were in relatively minor courts (Berkson, 1982). It was not until 1979 that every state had at least one female judge or justice of the peace. In 1965 Lorna Lockwood was appointed the first woman chief justice of a state supreme court, and in 1981 Sandra Day O'Connor was appointed the first female associate justice of the U.S. Supreme Court.

Access to the judiciary has also been limited by the highly political nature of judicial appointments in this country. Most judges are either elected by the public or appointed, and each system requires political connections and support. This has been particularly detrimental to women, who did not gain the constitutional right to vote until 1920 and did not become active in politics on a large scale until the 1970s. Even politically active women may find themselves at a disadvantage. At the federal level, for example, candidates with at least 15 years of legal experience are preferred, severely limiting the number of qualified women (Ness, 1982).

As more women practice law and recognize the importance of political activism, we can expect the number of female judges to increase. Their numbers are already growing, most probably as a response to a social environment more supportive of women in positions of authority and as a result of affirmative action legislation. Studies of female judges at both the state and federal levels suggest a growing belief that their sex helped them obtain a judgeship (Carbon, Houlden and Berkson, 1982).

While the drive to increase the number of female judges has resulted in appointees who are younger and less active in party politics than their male colleagues (Martin, 1982; Carbon, Houlden and Berkson, 1982), there are no indications that the quality of judicial appointments has suffered. In fact, procedures which reduce the influence of extraneous factors (such as race or sex) may also help focus greater attention on merit, thereby improving the quality of judicial appointments.

It is clear that women are making major inroads into the legal profession, particularly since the early 1970s. Continued progress can be continued for so long as the primary gatekeepers—law schools—actively encourage female enrollments. The time when the number of female attorneys equals that of males may not be far off, but it will be a much longer time before there is equality among law school professors or judges. It may take several generations for women to work their way up the status hierarchy, and that assumes no major periods of retrenchment, or reversals in policies aimed at fostering affirmative action. Despite this progress, there is clear evidence that discrimination against women still exists. It is also sadly ironic that the doors to law schools are opening to women at precisely the time when lawyers may be facing a saturated job market.

## Women in Policing

The situation of women in policing differs radically from that of women in law. In 1905, when 38 states had women lawyers, Lola Baldwin became the first sworn police officer with the powers of arrest (Walker, 1977). By 1985, when half of the new admissions to many law schools were female, less than 7 percent of all sworn police officers were women.

During the first two-thirds of this century, the place of women in policing was tenuous at best. Their numbers tended to swell during periods of war, when suitable males were in short supply, but nearly disappear in post-war periods (Price and Gavin, 1982). Until the 1970s, policewomen tended to serve in specialized functions consistent with their role as women. They worked primarily with juveniles, female offenders, female victims, vice assignments, and community relations. Many early policewomen took a strong social work orientation and saw their role as distinct from that of male officers. Some departments even established separate women's bureaus (Martin, 1980). While such specializations gave women a relatively uncontroversial entree to an otherwise masculine profession, working in these specialties also extracted a price. These women were often excluded from activities, such as routine patrol, which were necessary for promotion. By defining their contributions as unique, they were also precluded from competing with men for advancements and rewards within the department. Further, "early policewomen faced many barriers, including higher entrance requirements, admission quotas, and separate promotion lists (Martin, 1980)." Most early policewomen had no desire to compete directly for male police roles. Many had college degrees and a background in social work, teaching, or nursing (Horne, 1980).

> These women considered themselves unique and different from their male counterparts. They viewed themselves as social service workers rather than "cops," and, as such, they brought a philosophy of social work and reform into law enforcement, which emphasized the helping and reform of troubled and delinquent women and children (Horne, 1980:29).

Thus, when the International Association of Policewomen was established in 1915, its primary purpose was to inform police departments of the unique contributions and special skills possessed by policewomen, rather than to stress equality between the sexes (Horne, 1980; Martin, 1980).

The first major breakthrough for women in policing did not come until 1968 when Indianapolis became the first city to assign women to routine patrol duty. Women were first admitted on an equal basis with men to the Secret Service in 1971, and the FBI in 1972 (Martin, 1980). Despite federal legislation prohibiting discrimination on the basis of sex, "few departments have made a total commitment to hire women and, after hiring, to utilize them in all police functions (Price and Gavin, 1982: 404)." By 1985, women comprised only 6.8 percent of sworn police officers in the U.S., although they made up 64 percent of the civilian personnel hired by police departments (U.S. Department of Justice, 1985:248).

Policing is not only an occupation traditionally held by males, but has an image of violence and general machismo which is antithetical to stereotypical views of women. While much police work is routine, danger is an ever-present possibility. In 1984, for example, approximately 16 percent of sworn officers were assaulted in the line of duty, and nearly one-third of these assaults resulted in personal injury to the officer (U.S. Department of Justice, 1984:38). Further, while the public is generally accepting of policewomen, there has been no groundswell of public support for hiring female officers. Pressures to hire women have primarily come from the federal government, which may withhold funding, but even these federal regulations are being called into question (Pear, 1985; Elsasser, 1985).

## Reactions of Male Officers

Police officers have an unusually strong sense of group identity and group loyalty. Line officers who feel their work is unappreciated by the public and police administrators must rely on other officers to provide support, advice and physical protection. This strong sense of camaraderie typically extends to their social lives when off duty. Thus, being rejected by fellow officers means being excluded from informal information networks, social support and training in the unwritten rules which drive every organization. Researchers have consistently found that one of the major barriers to policewomen is their rejection by male officers, and one study of female officers found that the negative attitudes of male officers were the single greatest source of stress for female officers (Wexler and Logan, 1983).

While some resistance by males may be seen at the training academy (Pike, 1985; Wexler and Logan, 1983), most problems for female officers begin when they leave the academy. The guidance of seasoned officers is an important way for rookies to learn the ropes of policing, but female officers often find they are excluded from these informal networks (Martin, 1980; Wexler and Logan, 1983). Further, some reports suggest that when men and women are partners, men frequently dominate the situation, driving the car and dictating watch activities, leaving females to do paperwork or serve as assistants (Remmington, 1983).

Males who oppose female police give a variety of reasons. They are often concerned about their own physical safety and that of the female officers, believing that women are too small and simply not psychologically stable enough to handle crisis situations (Breece and Garrett, 1975; Charles, 1981; Martin, 1980; Milton, 1978). It is difficult to know how much of this concern derives from realistic fears of physical danger and how much of it derives from stereotypical images of women. Several studies, for example, suggest that some males adopt a protective attitude toward female officers (Breece and Garrett, 1975; Koenig, 1978; Milton, 1978).

Other males show concerns about the "sexually charged" nature of male/female patrols. For patrol situations where long hours may be spent with relatively little direct supervision, there is always the possibility of romantic involvement, or of unfounded allegations of such involvement. Given this, it should not be surprising that the *wives* of male officers also have strong reservations about hiring policewomen (Koenig, 1978; Milton, 1978).

Finally, many police officers are not only upset about the presence of women *per se*, but are concerned about the possibility that women are given preferential treatment in hiring, assignments, and promotion (Weisheit, in press).  For example, one survey of 191 male state police officers found that 71 percent thought there were more opportunities for women than for men in policing and 83 percent thought that women who were not efficiently performing their duties would be treated more leniently than men with the same problem.[1]  Table 6.1 shows that while there are reservations about women's performance, there are also respects in which women are believed to outperform men, such as their ability to deal with individuals involved in traffic accidents.  The most widely shared concerns, however, tend to focus on perceived inequities in the treatment of women by police agencies.  As one officer put it:

> From my point of view in the last two years it appears female troopers are getting better treatment than male troopers.  Quick stripes and most other departments chase after them like a dog in heat, either trying to impress them, or just enjoying their company....If you're female everybody opens closed doors, to ensure instant job openings.

Male officers were also concerned about their perception that females were less committed to policing.  As Table 6.1 shows, 80 percent of the male officers thought that women had less career commitment than men.  In fact, women were more likely to report they would quit before retirement, but this should not be surprising in light of friction with male officers and family demands which might arise if the woman decides to have children (Weisheit, in press).

## Public Reaction

Given media depictions of police work as dangerous and almost exclusively masculine, it might be expected that the public would also have serious reservations about policewomen.  Since most police activity is in response to citizen complaints, such reservations might hinder police work by undermining citizen confidence in the police, making them reluctant to call for assistance. Available evidence shows general public support for women as police officers.  In fact, Sherman (1973) suggests that citizens may be even more cooperative with policewomen than with policemen.  Kerber, Andes and Mittler (1977) found that most citizens had no preference for having a male or female come to their aid, thought that both males and females should be hired, and saw no differences in the expected leniency of male and female officers.  The only clear situation in which most preferred male officers involved cases of violence.

Table 6.1
Responses of 191 State Police Officers
to Statements about Policewomen.[1]

| Statement | Percent Agreeing |
|---|---|

PERFORMANCE
Female officers are probably better than male officers at dealing with people involved in traffic accidents.    92.7

Female officers will be more likely to panic in tense situations than will male officers.    56.9

Female officers are probably better than male officers at calming highly agitated individuals.    70.5

Female officers have to work harder than male officers to get proper credit for their work.    76.4

PREFERENTIAL TREATMENT
Female recruits have an easier time than males during training at the academy.    52.7

Female officers are more likely to get special job assignments because of their sex.    83.7

Females are more likely to get promotions because of their sex.    90.6

If it weren't for legal and government pressure, few police departments would hire many female officers.    94.8

MALE RESISTANCE
Female officers have a difficult time being accepted by male officers.    65.3

The extensive use of female officers will increase the likelihood of interpersonal conflict within a police department.    65.3

Female officers won't show as much of a long-term or career commitment to policing as male officers.    80.6

Many male officers would resent being supervised by a female officer.    85.3

Source: See Note 1.

## Police Administrators

Relatively little is known about how police administrators view female officers. It is interesting to note that, in 1986, when the U.S. Department of Justice threatened to bring charges against police departments with affirmative action quotas, several chiefs from major metropolitan departments staunchly defended affirmative action and expressed their intention to continue using quotas in hiring minority and female applicants ("Indy leans liberally," 1985). This attitude may be partly attributed to the valuable contribution made by female officers, but is more likely the result of concerns about lawsuits based on the failure to hire women and minority applicants. Walker (1985:555), has noted that "many, if not most of the major police departments have been sued over police discrimination." In addition, there are wide variations in the extent to which departments have hired females and minority officers. It is likely that large metropolitan departments, which are the usual sources of data, may more aggressively pursue female and minority applicants. But large departments are not typical of police departments nationwide. In fact, only one-half of one percent of the 11,912 police agencies in the U.S. are in cities with populations of 250,000 or more. Further, 63 percent of sworn officers in the U.S. work in cities or towns with populations less than 250,000 (U.S. Department of Justice, 1985:245). Unfortunately, much of what we know about women in policing comes from research on large urban departments where there are enough female officers that some mutual support is possible. In small departments, where there may be only 1 or 2 women, the problems faced by these women and the reactions of male officers may be quite different.

For administrators, increasing the number of female officers is a difficult task. In addition to the problem of resistance by male officers, there are relatively few qualified women who apply for police positions. The image of policing as a masculine occupation is pervasive in our society and nearly all departments receive far more applications from males than from females. It might be expected that as more women are hired and serve as visible reminders that police work is available to women, the number of female applicants will grow. Further, highly skilled female officers are much sought after and may transfer to other departments or to private firms.

## Redefining the Police Role

Hiring women may alter the police role in a number of ways. For example, many of the physical fitness tests usually used by departments to screen applicants focus on upper-body strength, placing women at a disadvantage.    Similarly, women more often have problems meeting minimum height and weight requirements.  A study in San Francisco found that 63% of male applicants but only 2 of 166 female applicants passed the physical agility test (Townsey, 1982).  The shortage of qualified female applicants is only made worse by these restrictive physical requirements.  In questioning the applicability of these requirements to females, departments have been forced to consider the importance of these tests for all officers.  There are doubts about whether these tests in any way relate to the kind of work actually done by police.  To date, no physical standards exist which have been shown essential for police work (Charles, 1981).  Some departments have separate standards for male and female applicants, while others have considered eliminating all but the most basic physical tests.  Separate standards may serve to perpetuate the image that women cannot "cut it" as real police officers while eliminating many aspects of physical fitness testing may seriously challenge conventional images of the demands of police work.

Questions about the importance of physical testing of police applicants ultimately involve questions about the use of physical force by the police.  Sherman (1973) has argued that female officers are better able to diffuse violence-prone situations and that the mere presence of women is often a social signal that the situation is not to be dealt with by violence.  Charles (1981) has noted that female recruits are less likely to view police work as a violent occupation in which physical force is essential.

Other research supports the idea that male and female officers may view the work differently.  While men are often attracted to police work because of the job security, women give a higher priority to the public service aspects of policing (Weisheit, in press).  And, both males and females are attracted to the relatively high salaries for a job requiring little prior training; females are likely to find the pay very high compared with more traditionally "female" occupations, such as waitressing or secretarial work (Ermer, 1978).

The use of female patrol officers has not only challenged traditional assumptions about police work, but examining the performance of these women has brought to the fore problems in the general assessment of police performance.  That is, if it is important to determine whether women are as capable as men of performing the police function, that function must be clearly stated and defined in measurable terms.  In their assessment of nine studies evaluating the performance of women on patrol, Morash and Greene (1986) argue that "performance" is so poorly and inconsistently defined that it is generally impossible to determine whether women satisfactorily perform police tasks.    They note a 2-phase study in Philadelphia, for example, where in phase one high performance scores were given for avoiding arrests while in phase two good performance was counted by the number of arrests made. The problem of comparing male and female performance is compounded by the fact that in some departments females are given "easier" assignments than males, even when the top administration explicitly mandates equality (Martin, 1980). Thus, many of the questions about women in policing are ultimately questions about policing itself, and about the manner in which male officers respond.

## Problems Specific to Women

In an occupation with a long tradition of hiring only males, policewomen find themselves confronted with special problems. The most obvious problem is the potential for conflict between family and work. Weisheit (in press), for example, found that 79 percent of the female officers in their study agreed that "Females are more likely than males to experience conflicts between the demands of their job and of their families." Part of the difficulty arises from the peculiar work hours, which may make child-care difficult, particularly for single mothers. In addition, the problem of maternity leave is a relatively new one for many departments, and those unwilling to grant extended leaves may force women to make a choice between their careers and their families (Weisheit, in press).

For male officers, traditional images of police work as a masculine occupation filled with risk and danger serves to reinforce their own masculinity. For women, however, traditional images of police work are in sharp conflict with traditional images of women. This conflict not only effects them on the job, but in their social life as well. Some report that other women and men outside of policing don't know how to respond to them. Others note that boyfriends, husbands, or family members strongly discouraged their decision to enter police work. Martin (1980) observed that policewomen resolved the incongruity of women having a masculine occupation in one of two ways. Some women emphasized their femininity, disliked working on the street, and saw police work as a source of income rather than as a long-term career. A few of these women even stated that women should not be allowed on patrol. Other women downplayed their femininity and defined themselves primarily as police. These women sought the same assignments as men, viewed policing as a career, and minimized differences between themselves and male officers. These women also minimized the effects of discrimination and were hostile to policewomen's organizations, which they saw as reaffirming male-female differences. For most women, choosing between an emphasis on their femininity and an emphasis on their skills as police officers is a no-win situation. Those who emphasize femininity are likely to be defined as inept officers, and those who emphasize their police skills are likely to have their femininity questioned.

Women have only recently been admitted as police officers, and resistance to them is still strong. The greatest barrier to accepting women in policing has not come from the public but from male officers. The stereotypical image of police work contrasts sharply with traditional images of women, leading many male officers to believe that women are incapable of effectively performing police work and that the status of the occupation is diminished by their presence. Female officers themselves must grapple with these conflicting images and the manner in which they resolve these conflicts has much to do with the way in which they approach the job.

As a group, female officers define police work differently than do male officers, focusing more on social service than crime fighting. While female officers will not change what police officers do, their presence has the potential to dramatically alter perceptions of police work, challenging the emphasis usually placed on violence and brute force. Further, their presence has led some to rethink what makes a "good" officer, and to question the meaning of the term "police performance."

## Women in Corrections

Women in corrections have faced many of the same problems as women in policing. Like women in policing, women have only recently been admitted to correctional occupations outside of those narrowly defined as "women's work" (e.g., work with juveniles or females). For many years, even these areas were considered unsuitable for women.

While there have been women prisoners in the U.S. for as long as there have been prisons, until the late 1800s there were few female guards, or matrons as they were first called. At first, female prisoners were housed in local jails or in separate rooms in men's prisons (Freedman, 1981; Rafter, 1985). In these facilities women were guarded exclusively by male officers; in some facilities they were visited by guards only at meal-time, and in others they were raped or forced into prostitution by male guards. In Indiana, for example, the prison administration itself operated a prostitution service for male guards, using the forced services of female inmates (Freedman, 1981:16).

While the first penitentiaries for men emphasized rehabilitation through solitude and hard work, most women were considered beyond reform. In addition, the very small number of female offenders made special work, treatment programs, or facilities expensive, which partly accounted for their mistreatment and neglect.

In the mid-1800s several events took place which led to the establishment of separate prisons for women which were directed and staffed primarily by women. First, during the Civil War, the crime rate for women rose at a much higher rate than for men. Their growing numbers made separate institutions for women more practical. Second, the mistreatment and sexual exploitation of female prisoners created embarrassing publicity for prison administrators, making the hiring of female guards for female inmates more justifiable. Third, many women gained valuable work experience during the Civil War and wanted to apply their skills outside the home following the war. Lobbying for and working in prisons for women was a logical choice for these women. Fourth, there was a growing sentiment that many women in prison were capable of reform and that males (often abusive husbands) were primarily responsible for their criminal activity. Therefore, female guards would be better than males at facilitating the reform of these women (Freedman, 1981).

The combination of these factors led to the first prison for women which opened in Indiana in 1874. Massachusetts first admitted women in 1877, and New York in 1887. Further, several American cities hired police matrons to supervise women in local jails and lockups between 1876 and 1888 (Freedman, 1981). Even in these early institutions there was a great reluctance on the part of male prison administrators to allow women to supervise female offenders, believing that women were simply not suited for controlling criminals of any kind. In most states, men continued to supervise women in local jails and in special sections of institutions for men. Nevertheless, the precedent had been set and by the turn of the century there was at least a begrudging acceptance of the idea that women could successfully guard other women. By 1975, only sixteen states did not have separate prisons for women (Freedman, 1981).

While the hiring of women to supervise female offenders opened some doors for professional women in corrections, it was a minor victory at best. The number of prisons for women is limited, with few states having more than one. In 1985, for example, women constituted only about four percent of the inmates housed in state and federal prisons (U.S. Department of Justice, 1986), and employment data for 1978 indicate that only 2.8 percent of all jobs in correctional institutions are in institutions for women (U.S. Department of Justice, 1981). Consequently, these institutions provide fewer job opportunities and more limited occupational mobility than in male institutions. For most of the history of prisons in this country, women were simply not allowed in positions which involved supervising male inmates.

It was not until 1972, when the 1964 Civil Rights Act was amended to include women under Title VII of the act, that women were granted the legal right to seek jobs as guards in men's prisons (Zimmer, 1986).[2]  This is the same legislation which provided the foundation for women to enter law and traditionally male police occupations.  Unfortunately, it is difficult to gauge the impact of the 1972 amendment.  While there are systematic counts of the number of female officers working in each state, these counts do not distinguish between women supervising female and those supervising male offenders.  Our best estimates of the number of female officers working in male institutions come from two studies, one conducted in 1979 and another in 1982.

In her survey of state departments of corrections, Morton (1979) found that women comprised approximately six percent of the officers in male institutions, while seventeen percent of the officers in women's prisons were men.  Over half of the states indicated Title VII of the Civil Rights Act was the main reason for hiring women in prisons for men.  Further, nine state agencies reported that more than 10 percent of the officer force in male facilities were women, with the highest percentages in Louisiana (18 percent), Wyoming (16 percent), and Kentucky (16 percent).  She found no major differences in the percentage of women in maximum, medium, and minimum security institutions.  Finally, 32 of the 49 responding states had no written policy regarding women guards.

A 1982 study by CONtact found an average of 8.4 percent of the officers in male institutions were female.  Further, most of the agencies reported that they restricted assignments by excluding female officers from inmate housing and other close contact assignments (CONtact, 1982 cited in Parisi, 1984).

Unfortunately, there is no system for routinely collecting data on the use of female officers in prisons for men, making it impossible to monitor changes and trends in employment patterns.  What data are available are collected by private agencies or individuals, and the cooperation of correctional agencies is always problematic.

## Legal Decisions

The situation of women in corrections differs from those in law and policing in several significant ways.  Working with male prisoners, particularly those convicted of sex offenses, raises issues about the safety of female officers.  In addition, the likelihood that guards will observe inmates taking showers and performing toilet functions raises serious constitutional questions about the privacy rights of male inmates.  While the courts have consistently upheld the right of women to work in law and policing, court rulings on women as correctional officers in male institutions have provided no consistent guidelines.  Examples of the legal confusion can be seen in several major court decisions, the most important of which is *Dothard v. Rawlinson* (1977).

In this case, Dianne Rawlinson was denied a job as a guard in an Alabama men's prison because she failed to meet the minimum weight requirements. While the case was pending, Alabama instituted a regulation barring women from all contact jobs in men's prisons, which she challenged as well. The court struck down the height and weight requirements as discriminatory, since prison officials could not demonstrate how these requirements were job-related. At the same time, the court upheld the state's ban on women guards in their maximum security prison because many sex offenders were housed there and because the court had, in 1976, ruled that the Alabama prisons were poorly managed and very dangerous. From the decision of the court, it appeared that women could not be precluded from working in other prisons for men unless similar conditions could be demonstrated by prison administrators. The Rawlinson case was the only case challenging the use of female guards in men's prisons to reach the Supreme Court and prison administrators have yet to successfully apply Rawlinson to situations in other states (Alpert, 1984; Jacobs, 1983; Zimmer, 1986). Thus, it is unclear from the Rawlinson decision when prisons for men are sufficiently dangerous to warrant restrictions on the hiring of female officers.

The cases which have followed *Rawlinson* have done little to clarify the role of female guards in men's prisons; some emphasize the right of women to work in institutions for men while others emphasize the privacy rights of inmates (Alpert, 1984; Jacobs, 1983; Parisi, 1984; Zimmer, 1986). For example, in *Gunther v. Iowa State Men's Reformatory* (1980), the court held that the dangerous conditions present in Alabama were not present in Iowa's medium security reformatories and concluded that correctional administrators must set policies which allow females to work as guards without invading the privacy of inmates using toilets. In *Forts v. Ward* (1980), the court held that although using male guards to supervise women in showers was an invasion of inmate privacy, males could be used elsewhere in the women's prison and that inmates have no constitutional right to supervision by guards of the same sex. Other cases allow females to conduct general "pat searches" of inmates but prohibit searches of the genital areas, except in emergencies. Again, however, what specifically constitutes an emergency is unclear from these court decisions (Peterson, 1982).

Thus, to satisfy equal opportunity requirements, women must be hired as guards in men's prisons, but to satisfy the inmates' privacy rights they may be restricted in their assignments. As Zimmer has noted (1986:9-10):

> For prison administrators the practical problems of sexual integration were exacerbated by the ambiguous (and ever-changing) legal situation and the failure of existing case law to clearly define women's proper employment role....Sexual integration has also caused administrative problems by decreasing management flexibility in deploying the guard force efficiently because although they have been forced to hire women, administrators have not been allowed, in most cases, to use them interchangeably with men. Every woman hired puts an additional constraint on managers' ability to assign personnel posts in the prison.

Further, although restrictions on their duties preclude a male prison staffed entirely by women, it is unclear what the "ceiling" should be on the number of women hired. Even when states set their own written hiring restrictions, these restrictions are often vague or confusing. Zimmer, for example, cites a state in which one administrator interpreted the guidelines as allowing women to bid for *only* 10 percent of the available posts while another interpreted the guidelines to mean that women could bid for *all but* 10 percent of the posts (Zimmer, 1986:86).

Thus, prison administrators and female guards are operating under vague and often contradictory legal guidelines. Unlike women in the law and women in policing, it is difficult to predict the long-term legal status of women as correctional officers in prisons for men. While it is likely that women will continue to be hired in these positions, restrictions on the assignments they may take make it likely that the courts eventually will have to confront questions about limitations on the number of women hired and their impact on the efficient operation of the prison.

Having established the legal context in which female guards have entered prisons for men, our attention now turns to the factors which motivate women to enter this highly unconventional occupation. Following this, we will examine issues surrounding their acceptance and performance as prison guards.

## Why Women Become Guards

Some might wonder why women would be interested in guarding male inmates. Two studies shed some light on this issue. In their study of male and female guards in a male institution, Jurick and Halemba (1984) found that males and females entered the occupation for different reasons. Over half of the women cited providing a service as their primary reason for entering the job while only twenty percent of the men gave this reason.

Females were more likely to cite *intrinsic* reasons for entering the job (e.g., inmate rehabilitation, human service work, beginning of career ladder) while males were more likely to focus on *extrinsic* factors (e.g., salary, job security, fringe benefits). While this study provided important insights, it focused on what males and females defined as the most attractive aspects of their jobs. It did not reveal the process by which women became aware of these job opportunities, defined themselves as viable candidates, and decided to actually apply. These issues were examined in a study by Zimmer (1986).

In her study of female guards in New York and Rhode Island, Zimmer (1986) found that a variety of factors drew women into guard positions in prisons for men. The first female guards in both states were those who used the union contract's seniority provisions to request a transfer from a female to a male institution. Usually they were seeking better posts and shifts, and in some cases prisons for males were closer to their homes, dramatically reducing commuting time. Others sought transfers for promotional opportunities, believing that experience in a major male institution was necessary for advancement into prison administration. None of the women she interviewed had aspired to be a guard from childhood, but some grew up with relatives or acquaintances who were prison guards, which may have removed some of the mystery of the work for them. Most came from traditional employment backgrounds in clerical work or waitressing and found that working in the prison was the highest paying job available. In many ways these women were very traditional in their sex-role attitudes. Only a few strongly supported the Equal Rights Amendment and more than half thought women with small children should not work outside the home. Most of these women had reservations about using women in high contact positions, and some even believed that women should not be allowed as guards in prisons for men. The majority of these women took the job with some apprehension and concern about their ability to perform effectively. In contrast to Jurick and Halemba (1984), Zimmer (1986:50) found that:

> If there is one generalization to be made about these women, it is that they become guards primarily because of extrinsic rewards—money, security and fringe benefits. In this respect, the women are probably quite similar to their male counterparts.

Combining the findings of Jurick and Halemba with those of Zimmer it appears that women apply for guard work in prisons for men out of economic necessity. At the same time, however, they value or emphasize different aspects of the job. Our attention now turns to the way their sex and approach to the job influence their acceptance by male guards and inmates.

## Acceptance by Male Guards

Female guards in prisons for men are likely to meet even stronger resistance from their male coworkers than women in policing. The resistance of male officers has probably been the single most studied aspect of women as guards. While there is a widespread belief among male officers that women simply do not belong in such jobs, the basis of these beliefs varies widely. Some officers are concerned about the safety of the women, and indicate a desire to shield or protect them from harm (Bowersox, 1981). At the same time, the belief that women are not fully capable of protecting themselves also implies that they cannot be depended on to protect or assist males in emergency situations (Kissel and Katsampes, 1980; Owen, 1985; Zimmer, 1986).

Males are also resentful of policies which give females highly preferred non-contact positions. In many prison systems, guards bid for these posts and are given them on the basis of seniority. Because of the privacy rights of inmates, however, relatively new females are often assigned such posts while male guards with considerable seniority are relegated to high-contact positions (Zimmer, 1986). Related to this is the belief that female officers will be promoted more rapidly, with less concern for their job performance than for their sex (Jurick, 1985; Owen, 1985).

The resistance of males must also be understood within the context of the changing prison environment. Legal requirements to hire women as guards in prisons for men occurred following nearly two decades of court decisions restricting the power of guards to control inmate behavior (Jacobs, 1980; Zimmer, 1986). Of course, guards have always relied heavily on the cooperation of inmates and on interpersonal skills, but court-ordered restrictions on such things as corporal punishment and administrative segregation diminished the extent to which guarding was officially recognized as requiring physical force. These restrictions also questioned the ability of guards to make proper decisions on their own. Thus, women were yet another symbol of the way in which the role was gradually being "emasculated."

Given their relatively small numbers and recent entrance into the occupation, it is too early to determine whether male animosity to female guards will diminish over time. At least one author has argued that while overt resistance may diminish, it may be substituted by more subtle forms of animosity and harassment (Peterson, 1982). For example, some women have reported that men with whom they work daily have never spoken to them, and others are excluded from lunch-room discussions and off-duty socializing (Zimmer, 1986:94-95). In addition, sexual rumors are often spread about female officers (Owen, 1985; Peterson, 1982), and these women are also subject to sexual harassment by male officers. All of the 70 female guards interviewed by Zimmer, for example, described at least one instance which could be described as sexual harassment, including one case in which a female officer received obscene calls from an inside line, and another in which the officer was repeatedly reminded of the sex crimes committed by inmates with whom she had direct contact (1986:94). Thus, while women have been officially recognized as suitable for guarding male inmates, it will probably be some time before they are fully accepted by male guards.

## Acceptance by Inmates

Male inmates have been generally accepting of female guards. Some prefer females, believing that female guards are easier to interact with, more sympathetic, and less punitive. It is also felt that female guards make the prison more like the outside world and prepare them for interactions with women upon their release (Jacobs, 1983; Kissel & Katsampes, 1980; Parisi, 1984; Peterson, 1982). Many of the female guards in Zimmer's (1986) study "...claimed that the inmates were kinder, more helpful, and more accepting of their presence than were male guards (p. 101)."

A few inmates object to the presence of females, citing concerns over privacy and resenting supervision by women. Even though females help normalize the atmosphere of the prison, their presence might also heighten sexual tensions of male inmates (Peterson, 1982). Like male guards, inmates were not prepared for the hiring of female guards and initial reactions included apprehension, rudeness and hostility. Also, like male guards, some inmates felt the need to protect female guards from aggressive or violent inmates (Zimmer, 1986).

Most inmates, however, are probably indifferent about the presence of female guards, believing that "a guard is a guard." While the entrance of women into the prison as guards may have been of some symbolic importance to inmates, it has had little effect on their day-to-day routine. Even if male and female guards differ in their interpersonal styles, their basic tasks remain the same. Further, in most male institutions the number of female guards is quite small and they are restricted to low-contact posts, minimizing their interactions with inmates.

## Contradictions Facing Female Guards

Women guards in prisons for men often find themselves facing contradictions. On the one hand, they may make unique contributions to the prison environment, including a feminine, "humanistic" approach to the job which may reduce inmate-guard tensions, and their presence makes the prison environment more similar to the outside world. On the other hand, these unique contributions come at a price:

> ...to the extent that females are hired to exhibit feminine characteristics, which nevertheless have a positive effect on inmates, parity in the correctional work force will suffer (Parisi, 1984:103).

Further, defining female officers as unique is likely to slow the process of their acceptance into the informal social network of guards, where much of the most valuable training and socialization takes place.

Another area of contradictions arises from job assignments. The advantages of being assigned the "easiest" jobs, may be offset by the fact that such jobs preclude women from obtaining the frontline experience required for rapid promotions. Although court orders protecting inmate privacy rights preclude women from working in some sections of maximum security prisons, these orders further reinforce the image that such women are not "real" guards. The underlying contradictions between the right of women to employment in correctional institutions and the right of inmates to some degree of privacy are not completely reconcilable. In this respect the problems of sexually integrating the prison guard force are likely to be more persistant than the problems of sexually integrating the police.

## Summary

There are many similarities among females entering law, policing, and corrections. In all three of these cases the greatest obstacle was not the performance or ability of the women, but the resistance of male co-workers. In each of these areas legislative and court actions were necessary before significant numbers of women were hired. In all three occupations the presence of women has challenged the importance of uniquely masculine aggressiveness and bravado for working in these positions. As we move from the legal system, through policing, and to corrections, the resistance of males has been greater, and the numbers of women smaller. However much these pioneering women have challenged the masculine images of these jobs, there is little evidence that they dramatically alter the nature of the organizations in which they work, or the manner in which work is carried out. By and large these women are professionals first and women second.

## Notes

[1] In the summer of 1985 surveys were sent to a random sample of 255 male state police officers and all 56 female officers. Two hundred thirty three surveys were returned, yielding a response rate of 75%. A fuller description of the data collection process and additional data can be found in Weisheit, (in press).

[2] See Chapman et al. (1983) for a thorough discussion of legislative mandates and restrictions regarding the hiring of women in corrections.

# References

Abramson, J., & Franklin, B. (1986). *Where they are now: The story of the women of Harvard Law 1974.* New York: Doubleday.

Alpert, G. (1984). The needs of the judiciary and misapplication of social research: The case of female guards in men's prisons. *Criminology, 22*(3), 441-456.

Berkson, L. (1982). Women on the bench: A brief history. *Judicature, 65*(6), 286-293.

Bodine, L. (1983). Sandra Day O'Connor. *American Bar Association Journal, 69*, 1394, 1396-1398.

Bowersox, M.S. (1981). Women in corrections: Competence, competition, and the social responsibility norm. *Criminal Justice and Behavior, 8*(4), 491-499.

Breece, C. & Garrett, G.R. (1975). The emerging role of women in law enforcement. In J. Kinton (Ed.). *Police roles in the seventies: Professionalization in America.* Aurora, IL: Social Science and Sociological Research.

Carbon, S., Houlden, P. & Berkson, L. (1982). Women on the state bench. *Judicature, 65*(6), 294-305.

Chapman, J.R., Minor, E.K., Rieker, P., Mills, T.L. & Bottum, M. (1983). *Women employed in corrections* (Grant No. 79-ED-AX-0011). Washington, D.C.: National Institute of Justice.

Charles, M.T. (1981). The performance and socialization of female recruits in the Michigan State Police Training Academy. *Journal of Police Science and Administration, 9*(2), 209-223.

Chester, R. (1985). *Unequal access: Women lawyers in a changing America.* South Hadley, MA: Bergin & Garvey Publishers, Inc.

Culver, J.H. & Wold, J.T. (1986). Rose Bird and the politics of judicial accountability in California. *Judicature, 70*(2), 81-89.

Curran, B.A. (1986).   American lawyers in the 1980s: A profession in transition. *Law and Society Review, 20*(1), 19-52.

*Dothard v. Rawlinson*, 433 U.S. 321,335 (1977).

Elsasser, G. (1985, May 7).   Justice Department fails to file data on hiring. *Chicago Tribune*, p. 4.

Epstein, C.F. (1981).   *Women in law*. New York: Basic Books.

Ermer, V.B. (1978).   Recruitment of female police officers in New York City. *Journal of Criminal Justice, 6*(3), 233-246.

Ex-chief of police, a woman, wins stress disability claim. (1986, October 23). *New York Times*, p. 18.

Faught, J.J. (1986).   Update:  The status of women faculty in Illinois law schools. *Illinois Bar Journal, 74*(9), 452-455.

*Forts v. Ward*, 434 F.Supp. 946 (S.D.N.Y.) rev'd and remanded, 566 F.2d 849 (2d Cir. 1977), on remand, 471 F.Supp. 1095 (1978), vacated in part 621 F.2d 1210 (1980).

Fossum, D. (1983).  Women in the law: A reflection on Portia. *American Bar Association Journal, 69*, 1389-1393.

Freedman, E.B. (1981).   *Their sisters' keepers: Women's prison reform in America, 1830-1930*. Ann Arbor, MI: University of Michigan Press.

*Gunther v. Iowa State Men's Reformatory*, 612 F.2d 1079 (8th Cir. 1980).

Horne, P. (1980).   *Women in law enforcement* (2nd ed.). Springfield, IL: Charles C. Thomas.

Indy leans liberally in quota war (1985, July 4).  *Chicago Tribune*, p. 3.

Jacobs, J.B. (1980).  The prisoners' rights movement and its impacts, 1960-80. In N. Moris and M. Tonry (Eds.), *Crime and justice: An annual review of research, Volume 2*. Chicago: University of Chicago Press.

Jacobs, J.B. (1983).   Female guards in men's prisons. In J.B. Jacobs (Ed.), *New perspectives on prisons and imprisonment*. Ithaca, NY: Cornell U. Press.

Jenkins, J.A. (1985, November).   The trouble with Rose Bird. *TWA Ambassador*, pp. 68-72, 74, 76, 78, 79, 82, 83.

Jurick, N.C. & Halemba, G.J. (1984).   Gender, working conditions and the job satisfaction of women in a nontraditional occupation: Female correctional officers in men's prisons. *The Sociological Quarterly, 25*(Autumn), 551-566.

Jurick, N. C. (1985).   An officer and a lady: Organizational barriers to women working as correctional officers in men's prisons. *Social Problems, 32*(4), 375-388.

Kerber, K. W., Andes, S. M., & Mittler, M. B. (1977).   Citizen attitudes regarding the competence of female officers. *Journal of Police Science and Administration, 5*(3), 337-347.

Kissel, P. J. & Katsampes, P. L. (1980).   The impact of women corrections officers on the functioning of institutions housing male inmates. *Journal of Offender Counseling, Services & Rehabilitation, 4*(3), 213-231.

Koenig, E.J. (1978).   An overview of attitudes toward women in law enforcement. *Public Administration Review, 38*(3), 267-275.

Lindsey, R. (1986, November 6).  Deukmejian and Cranston win as 3 judges ousted. *The New York Times*, p. 16.

Martin, E. (1982).  Women on the federal bench. *Judicature, 65*(6), 306-313.

Martin, S.E. (1980).  *Breaking and entering: Policewomen on patrol.* Berkeley: University of California Press.

McFadden, R.D. (1981, June 7).   Two-time murderer accused of slaying prison guard. *The New York Times*, p. 37.

McNamara, P.H. (1986).   A followup on Hinshon: Will the partnership process change as more women enter law firms? *Illinois Bar Journal, 74*(9), 430-434.

Milton, C.H. (1978).   The future of women in policing. In A. W. Cohen (Ed.). *The future of policing.* Beverly Hills, CA: Sage.

Morash, M. & Greene, J.R. (1986). Evaluating women on patrol: A critique of contemporary wisdom. *Evaluation Review, 10*(2), 230-255.

Morton, J.B. (1979). Women in correctional employment: Where are they now and where are they headed? [Summary]. *Proceedings of the One Hundred and Ninth Annual Congress of Correction of the American Correctional Association*, 255-262.

Ness, S. (1982). A sexist selection process keeps qualified women off the bench. In B.R. Price and N.J. Sokoloff (Eds.). *The criminal justice system and women.* New York: Clark Boardman.

New York Task Force on Women in the Courts (1986). *Report of the New York Task Force on Women in the Courts.* New York, NY: Office of Court Administration.

O'Neill, P. (1986, June 3). Controversy, national acclaim marks of Harrington's career. *Portland Oregonian.* p. 11.

Owen, B.A. (1985). Race and gender relations among prison workers. *Crime and Delinquency, 31*(1), 147-159.

Parisi, N. (1984). The female correctional officer: Her progress toward and prospects for equality. *The Prison Journal, 64*(1), 92-109.

Pear, R. (1985, October 15). White House plan would ease job-bias rules. *Chicago Tribune*, p. 1,16.

Peterson, C.B. (1982). Doing time with the boys: An analysis of women correctional officers in all-male facilities. In B. R. Price and N. Sokoloff (Eds.), *The criminal justice system and women.* New York: Clark Boardman.

Pike, D.L. (1985). Women in police academy training: Some aspects of organizational response. In I.L. Moyer (Ed.) The changing roles of women in the criminal justice system. Prospect Heights, Il: Waveland Press.

Portland's tarnished Penny (1986, April 14). *Time*, p. 26.

Price, B.R. & Gavin, S. (1982). A century of women in policing. In B.R. Price and N. Sokoloff (Eds.), *The criminal justice system and women.* New York: Clark Boardman.

Rafter, N. (1985). *Partial justice: Women in state prisons, 1800-1935.* Boston: Northeastern University Press.

Remmington, P. W. (1983). Women in the police: Integration or separation. *Qualitative Sociology, 6*(2), 118-135.

Saxon, W. (1981, May 17). Female prison guard found slain in Dutchess County. *The New York Times*, p. 31.

Sherman, L.J. (1973). A psychological view of women in policing. *Journal of Police Science and Administration, 1*(4), 383-394.

Townsey, R.D. (1982). Female patrol officers: A review of the physical capability issue. In B.R. Price & N.J. Sokoloff (Eds.). *The criminal justice system and women*. New York: Clark Boardman.

U.S. Bureau of the Census (1985). *Statistical Abstract of the United States: 1986.* (196th edition). Washington, D.C.: U.S. Government.

U.S. Department of Justice (1981). *Expenditure and employment data for the criminal justice system, 1978.* Washington, D.C.: U.S. Government Printing Office.

U.S. Department of Justice (1984). *Law enforcement officers killed and assaulted.* Washington, D.C.: U.S. Government Printing Office.

U.S. Department of Justice (1985). *Uniform crime reports.* Washington, D.C.: U.S. Government Printing Office.

U.S. Department of Justice (1986). *State and Federal Prisoners, 1925-85.* Washington, D.C.: U.S. Government Printing Office.

Walker, S. (1977). *A critical history of police reform.* Lexington, M.A.: Lexington Books.

Walker, S. (1985). Racial minority and female employment in policing. *Crime and Delinquency, 31*(4), 555-572.

Weisberg, D.K. (1977). Barred from the bar: Women and legal education in the United States, 1870-1890. *Journal of Legal Education, 28*(4), 485-507.

Weisberg, D.K. (1979). Women in law school teaching: Problems and progress. *Journal of Legal Education, 30*(1-2), 226-248.

Weisheit, R.A. (in press). Women in the state police: Concerns of male and female officers. *Journal of Police Science and Administration.*

Wexler, J.G. & Logan, D.D. (1983). Sources of stress among women police officers. *Journal of Police Science and Administration, 11*(1), 46-53.

Winter, B. (1983). Survey: Women lawyers work harder, are paid less, but they're happy. *American Bar Association Journal, 69*, 1384-1388.

Zimmer, L.E. (1986). *Women guarding men.* Chicago: University of Chicago Press.

# Author Index

# Subject Index

Abortion 53
Affirmative action 146, 151
    (*see also* Discrimination)
Age 10, 11, 14, 17, 19, 33, 45, 53, 55, 56, 66, 70, 78, 106, 143
Alcohol
    (*see* Drugs)
American Bar Association 140, 142, 143
Assault 5, 7, 8, 33, 55, 89, 99-100
Australia 35, 42
Battering 88, 90, 102-106, 109
Biological factors 11-15
Birth control
    (*see* Pregnancy)
Burglary 2, 5, 6-8, 40
Children 10-11, 18-19, 21, 43, 53-54, 57, 65-66, 70, 74, 92-98,
    103-105, 142, 147, 149, 153, 159
Chivalry 52, 54
Civil Rights Act 155
Correctional officers
    (*see* Guards)
Crimes
    Index crimes 6-7
    Property crimes 3-7, 11, 19, 22, 36-37, 42, 66, 70
    Self-report studies 6, 10, 19, 42
    Victimless crimes 5
    Violent crimes 2, 5-6, 11, 13, 15, 19, 22, 31, 36, 40, 96, 97
    (*see also* specific offenses)
Death penalty 29-30, 55
Discrimination 52-56
    by courts 41, 51, 55, 56, 143
    employment 21, 106-108, 138, 146-147, 149, 154, 157
    in law 53, 56